101
BEST AUSTRALIAN
BEACHES

www.101bestbeaches.com

101 BEST AUSTRALIAN BEACHES

ANDY SHORT | BRAD FARMER

NEWSOUTH

A NewSouth book

Published by

NewSouth Publishing
University of New South Wales Press Ltd
University of New South Wales
Sydney NSW 2052
AUSTRALIA
newsouthpublishing.com

First published 2012

10 9 8 7 6 5 4 3 2 1

National Library of Australia Cataloguing-in-Publication entry
Author: Short, Andrew D.
Title: 101 best Australian beaches/Andrew D. Short and Brad Farmer.
ISBN: 978 174223 322 2 (pbk.)
ISBN: 978 174224 112 8 (ePub)
ISBN: 978 174224 599 7 (ePDF)
Notes: Includes index.
Subjects: Beaches – Australia.
        Bathing beaches - Australia.
Other Authors/Contributors: Farmer, Brad.
Dewey Number: 919.4

Design Josephine Pajor-Markus
Cover Rainbow Beach, Queensland. Courtesy of Tourism Queensland.
Printer 1010 Printing

This book is printed on paper using fibre supplied from plantation or
sustainably managed forests.

INTRODUCTION

The thin strips of sand where land meets sea have always fascinated humans. The beach is where life first crawled out of the oceans, where people have hunted, feasted and played for thousands of years, and where many different cultures have first encountered one another, peacefully or otherwise.

Shorelines are dynamic, ever-changing places. Washed clean twice a day by the incoming tide, beaches are also constantly being reshaped by the forces of wind and water. Shorelines shift, cliffs collapse, tidal pools fill and empty. On land and in the water, plants provide shelter and food for a dazzling array of life.

Australia has no fewer than 11 761 beaches along its 30 000-kilometre coast. We have been to every one of them, as well as hundreds more on our offshore islands. Both of us are keen surfers who have been travelling our coastline in search of a break since we were teenagers, with one of us also a marine scientist who has investigated every one of Australia's mainland beaches.

No other country has such a varied shoreline, from the palm-shaded beaches of the tropical north, to the wild wave-washed southern shores.

The Southern Ocean is the world's greatest wave factory, providing year-round swell that pounds the southern half of the continent, while strong onshore winds build massive coastal sand dunes. This temperate oceanic zone is rich in marine life, from whales and their annual migration to the world's largest temperate seagrass meadows that stretch from Port Phillip Bay in

Victoria to Shark Bay in Western Australia.

The northern tropical coast is cooled by balmy trade winds and lower waves but it also has to cope with seasonal cyclones and the huge tides that reach 10 metres in the northwest. The northern coast is also fringed by mangroves, tropical seagrasses and the world's largest coral reef, the Great Barrier Reef, and is home to dugongs, turtles and crocodiles.

Aboriginal people – saltwater people – have lived near, harvested and enjoyed this extraordinary shoreline for thousands of years as attested by the middens and rock carvings that are found along the coast. We know that their experiences were deeply connected spiritually to the beaches through Dreamtime stories and their cultural connections are still strong today. European settlers were perhaps slower to appreciate the delights of the beach: in fact, Victorian-era modesty led to sea bathing being outlawed in daylight hours until the 1900s (see Bondi).

We've certainly changed since then. The coastline, and the beach culture that has grown up along it, defines Australia perhaps more than any other modern nation. Not only are we blessed with the world's best and best managed beaches (see Why we have the world's best beaches), but we are also lucky that they have remained such egalitarian spaces, open to everybody. Our beaches are not only priceless but also free. While Europeans gather in town squares, Australians choose the sand to view, sunbake, wade, swim, surf, fish and compete, while our famous surf life savers are on hand to assist those overcome by the power of the surf.

In this book, we have taken on the difficult task of identifying the very best of our 11 761 beaches. To do that, we looked at every beach and at the factors that make beaches special – the views, the sand, surf, bordering headlands and a range of supporting amenities. We looked for the best natural experiences, but also for great city beaches and for those with fascinating historical or human stories.

And then we sat down and debated which of the thousands of wonderful beaches should make the final cut. We hit the road again to check out the beaches on our long list so that we could whittle it down to the final 101. We didn't always agree – Andy, a scientist, tended to focus on fascinating geological features while Brad would be rhapsodising over the sheer beauty of the place or a single shell. Somehow though, in spite of there being only one overlap in our personal top 10s, we did manage to come up with a final list that we both believe represents the best of the best – and we did it without coming to blows.

Not everybody will agree with our selection, of course. Most Australians probably have their favourite beach and some will be outraged to find theirs has been overlooked. To them we say, the 11 660 runners-up are also worth exploring. Whether you're a surfer, angler, beachcomber, or you just like building sandcastles with the kids, the beach has something for everyone.

WHY WE HAVE THE WORLD'S BEST BEACHES

The island-continent of Australia boasts the world's best beaches – a big claim but one we feel confident is justified. And there are several reasons why.

First, there's the nature of the coast. Although Australia does have a few very long beaches, the coastline is dominated by thousands of small bays, headlands, reefs and islets creating attractive seascapes along most parts of the coast.

A key factor in creating a great beach is sand – the size and nature of the sand grains helps determine colour, slope and width, as well as the nature of the surf zone and its rips and bars. Australian beaches have some of the best and cleanest sand in the world. About half of all our beaches have clean white to yellow quartz sand that ultimately comes from the ancient granite rocks of the interior. Added to this is carbonate detritus (the pulverised remains of shells and other marine life), which adds its own colours and texture. The continental shelf along our southern shores has the world's largest temperate seagrass meadows and is the largest carbonate producer in the world, producing the abundance of detritus that has helped to build the most massive beaches and coastal dunes in the world.

Then there's the water. We have a mostly arid climate so the continent has few rivers, a situation that has existed for the past 40 million years. The absence of rivers means there is not much fine silt and mud entering the ocean so we get clear water over those clean white-yellow sands.

Our oceans also deliver the waves that provide much of the drama, and recreational opportunities, at our beaches. The great Southern Ocean provides regular surf to the southern coast year-round.

Added to this is the diversity of our plant and animal life and the fact that most of the beaches are in a natural state, many of them protected by national parks or other reserves. The net result is thousands of pristine undeveloped beaches with clear water, clean sand and surf, usually bordered by headlands and reefs and backed by vegetated coastal dunes, in climates that range from tropical to temperate.

The Australian love affair with the beach has led huge numbers of us, including the authors of this book, to become campaigners for the preservation of our coast. Many of the beaches in this book would not have retained their natural magic without vigilant community engagement to ensure sensitive coastal planning and conservation. If you love the beach, we urge you to get involved in coastal and marine protection to make sure future generations can continue to enjoy the world's best beaches.

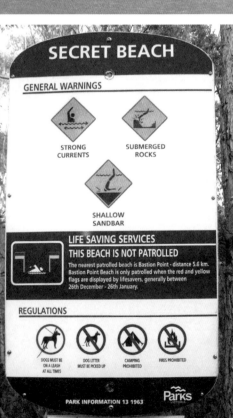

BEACH SAFETY

Australia has a wide variety of beaches, from those with wide tidal flats and almost no waves to those dominated by massive waves and rip currents. So when going to the 'beach' be aware of what type of beach you are going to.

The fact that Australia has 310 surf life saving clubs, plus more than 150 beaches patrolled by lifeguards, shows that there are various types of dangers associated with beaches. By taking a few simple steps you can easily avoid getting into trouble.

Most of the 12 000 beach rescues in Australia each year occur as a result of rip currents, fast-moving currents that move seaward through the surf zone. They occur on *all* beaches where waves are breaking and there is surf. If you want to avoid rips, try not to go deeper than waist depth so that you can wade against a strong current. If you want to really immerse yourself, never swim alone and swim only at a patrolled beach between the red and yellow flags. Even then, stay on the bar or in shallow water and keep away from deeper channels, troughs or strong currents. Remember if the water is moving sideways it's heading for a rip, if it's moving seaward, you're *in* a rip!

If you find yourself in a rip current, don't panic, but float and raise one hand to signal for help while trying to move away from the main current. If there is no help stay calm, conserve your energy and when the current weakens calmly swim or let the waves wash you to shore. Remember a rip current will not drown you, but panic will.

Rips are just one concern. All beaches are exposed to the sun and to avoid sunburn observe the simple rule – Slip (on a T-shirt), Slop (on sunscreen) and Slap (on a hat). Those are the 3 S's to be followed, then there are the six S's to be avoided, particularly in the tropical north: Stingers, Sea snakes, Stonefish, Stingrays, Sharks and Salties (crocodiles). Observe warning signs and remember that it is always best to swim at patrolled beaches in stinger enclosures, especially during summer.

Despite all the hazards, Australia has one of the lowest rates of beach rescues in the world. This is largely the result of swimming programs, beach safety education, a 'beach aware' population and the world-class life saving and lifeguarding services that patrol popular beaches year-round.

Some of our 101 best beaches are hazardous, as indicated in the text. These are to be visited, viewed, photographed, walked and enjoyed, but are not necessarily the best place for a swim.

Lastly, don't swim at night, alone, or under the influence of alcohol or drugs!

ADVENTURE BAY BRUNY ISLAND, TASMANIA

ISLAND BEACH | SEAFARING HISTORY | SPECTACULAR LOOKOUT | ECO BOAT TOURS

The sandy isthmus connecting the two halves of Bruny Island forms the southern boundary of historic Adventure Bay, which was visited by an honour roll of 18th-century European navigators. Climb the long staircase to the top of the dunes for a 360-degree panoramic view, or take an eco boat tour along the island's dramatic coastline.

Adventure Bay on Tasmania's Bruny Island boasts an honour roll of visiting early navigators that must surely be unrivalled by any other beach in the country. It was here that in 1642 Abel Tasman tried to find shelter; where Tobias Furneaux stayed after becoming separated from Captain James Cook's ship in 1773; and where Cook (1777), Captain William Bligh and his *Bounty* (1788 and pre-mutiny of course!) and the French explorers, Joseph-Antoine D'Entrecasteaux (1792) and Nicolas Baudin (1802) all laid anchor.

Just south of Hobart, the island is best accessed by the 15-minute sweep across the D'Entrecasteaux Channel on the car ferry from Kettering.

Bruny is really an island of two parts, precariously connected by a 7-kilometre-long – and in places only 50-metre-wide – sandy isthmus, known as The Neck. And, although it is the same size as Singapore, the island has only 700 residents enjoying its 234 kilometres of shoreline – including 94 varied beaches. There is a lot to see and do here: camping, fishing, surfing, admiring the fur seal colonies and pods of dolphins, and hiking and touring the rugged southern coast.

Adventure Bay is the largest community on the island strung out along a curved north-facing beach and offering a range of activities, including eco boat tours. A small museum honours the bay's rich seafaring history. The beach is generally calm, particularly at the southern end, with waves slowly increasing in size as you move up the bay. Stop at The Neck lookout on the spectacular sandy isthmus where you'll find a monument to Truganini, who lived at the Aboriginal mission here in the 1820s, and (at the top of the long staircase to the crest of a sand dune) a 360-degree panoramic view. In the south, densely forested slopes rise 500 metres to the South Bruny Range and 250 metres to the eastern headland, Fluted Cape.

Two other beaches worth visiting while on the island are Cloudy Bay, for surf and the nearby lighthouse, and Jetty Beach, for a quiet, safe beach with camping in the coastal bush behind.

MOST HISTORIC

A few Australian beaches have a very early association with European exploration and settlement:

» Jakes Beach, WA – two sailors were set ashore here in 1629 as punishment for their part in the *Batavia* mutiny and were never heard of again

» Adventure Bay, TAS – many maritime explorers visited here including Abel Tasman (1642), Tobias Furneaux (1773), James Cook (1777), William Bligh (1788), Joseph-Antoine D'Entrecasteaux (1792) and Nicolas Baudin (1802)

» Manly Beach, NSW – named by Arthur Phillip in 1788 after the 'manly' Aborigines

» Emily Bay, Norfolk Island – site of the First Fleet's second settlement in 1788

At least 50 beaches are named after shipwrecks with many more first visited by the early sealers, timber-getters and fishermen.

AGNES WATER

OCEAN SUNSETS | SUPERB ESTUARY | ECO TOURS | SITE OF COOK'S SECOND LANDFALL

Quiet Agnes Water boasts the northernmost surf in Queensland, although it's usually on the gentle side. Explore the superb estuary, neighbouring national parks or head offshore to the southern outposts of the Great Barrier Reef.

Nomadic surfers visit this quaint village for the northernmost surf in Queensland, but most people are drawn to Agnes Water for its superb beach and estuary.

Until the 1970s, this isolated outpost was a well-guarded secret: a few lonely beach shacks stood at the end of the rough 50-kilometre-long track cut by creek crossings. It's a bit easier to get to today, but this stretch of coast still feels remarkably isolated and pristine, with much of it protected in the Deepwater and Eurimbula national parks.

Agnes Water's most famous visitor was Captain James Cook, who dropped anchor here in 1770, just a month after his historic Botany Bay landing. This was Cook's second landfall on the Australian continent and he spent two days anchored in the place he named Bustard Bay, investigating deserted Aboriginal camps and noting the more tropical flora and fauna and increased tidal range compared with down south. The visit is commemorated in the Joseph Banks

Conservation Area (named for Cook's naturalist) at the northern end of the beach.

Occasional higher swell brings surf to the southern end and waves and rips along the beach, but generally you will find low waves breaking over a shallow sandbar. Around the northern Round Hill Head is Bustard Bay and Round Hill Creek, both part of Eurimbula National Park, followed by 20 kilometres of long sandy beaches all the way to Bustard Head, site of Queensland's first mainland lighthouse. Eco-tours run to all these areas from Agnes Water.

If you have a boat, you can fish the extensive estuary of Round Hill inlet or head 50 kilometres out to sea to visit Fitzroy Reef and Lady Musgrave Island the southernmost outposts of the Great Barrier Reef.

In the evening, wander down to the water's edge to see the glorious deep orange sunset over Bustard Bay, one of the few places on the east coast of Australia where you can watch the sun set over water.

AVOCA BEACH NEW SOUTH WALES

ROCK PLATFORMS | TIDAL POOLS | SURFING | LAGOON | HISTORIC PICTURE THEATRE

With its golden strip of gently curving sand and prominent sandstone headlands, Avoca Beach is the pick of the beaches on the NSW Central Coast. The beach blocks the mouth of Avoca Lake, a small estuarine lagoon that occasionally breaks out across the sand (avoca is a Celtic word meaning 'great estuary' or 'river mouth'). With its headlands, rock platforms, surf, pools and lagoon, this delightful beach has something for everyone.

Development started at the southern end of the beach after a bridge was built across the lake in 1908. A surf life saving club followed in 1929. This is still the most popular part of the beach, with usually good surf (including the southern point break), a sheltered rock pool for wading and swimming and a rock platform leading part way round the headland where you can see some interesting rock formations. It offers visitors a range of accommodation and restaurants, along with the surf club, shady Hunter Park and an historic beachside picture theatre.

Quieter North Avoca was developed from the 1950s and is mainly residential, with a surf life saving club founded in 1957.

There is good surf right along the beach, but because of the rips you should only swim in patrolled areas or in the tidal pool. The lagoon is popular for swimming, fishing and canoeing around its mostly unspoilt shoreline.

Sandstone headlands, rock platforms, surf, tidal pools and an estuarine lagoon mean Avoca Beach on the NSW Central Coast has something for everyone.

BALMORAL BEACH
SYDNEY, NEW SOUTH WALES

URBAN CAFE LIFE | TIDAL POOL | HISTORIC BATHING PAVILION | ABORIGINAL MIDDENS

Directly opposite the majestic entrance to Sydney Harbour, sheltered Balmoral Beach has long been a favourite destination for Sydneysiders thanks to its mix of urban café lifestyle, clear blue water and netted swimming beach.

Crescent-shaped Balmoral Beach must surely be one of the world's most beautiful city beaches. Directly opposite the majestic entrance to Sydney Harbour, Balmoral includes the northern Edwards Beach, separated from its longer neighbour by Rocky Point, which is connected to the mainland by a sandy tombolo and elaborate footbridge. The footbridge and equally decorative rotunda in the adjoining park were built in the 1930s when daytrippers used to arrive by ferry from Circular Quay.

Together, the two beaches sweep in an east-facing arc of white sand, fronting calm waters or a lazy ocean swell washing through the heads. Edwards Beach houses the Balmoral Beach (swimming) Club, founded in 1914, whose members can be seen swimming laps of the beach every morning of the year. The former grand bathing pavilion, built in 1928, now houses The Bathers' Pavilion restaurant. Edwards also has a small northern rock pool and larger netted pool in the southern corner for those concerned about

Sydney Harbour's sharks. Above the northern pool, stood a stepped amphitheatre built in the 1920s by a theosophical group to welcome Christ as he floated through the heavenly heads of Sydney Harbour.

The longer southern stretch of beach is interrupted by a central rock reef, beyond which Sydney's largest and most popular tidal pool curves 100 metres out into the bay. Scores of pleasure craft moor between the pool and the southern point, on whose wooded slopes stands the naval base, HMAS *Penguin*. Behind this part of the beach, is the large Balmoral Park with caves and Aboriginal middens attesting to the long human presence on these shores.

Balmoral is a place where many northern Sydneysiders head for an early dip or coffee, for walks, a barbecue or picnic lunch, for swimming, boating, yachting and a range of related water activities, including a popular access site for scuba divers. It's always busy with much to do on the land and in the harbour.

BEST ROCK POOL & SWIMMING CLUB

Many New South Wales beaches have rock pools at one or both ends. Some of the best pools, and their names, or swimming clubs, are:

» South Curl Curl, NSW – Frigid Frogs
» North Narrabeen, NSW – Shivering Sharks
» South Bondi, NSW – Bondi Icebergs
» Coogee, NSW – Ladies Pool
» Bermagui, NSW – Blue Pool
» Newcastle, NSW – Bogey Hole (excavated by convicts in 1820)

All rock pools take advantage of the natural rock formations and tidal flushing and in big seas they may be literally swamped.

BELLS BEACH GREAT OCEAN ROAD, VICTORIA

SURFING HERITAGE | POWERFUL SOUTHERN OCEAN WAVES | SPECTACULAR COASTAL DRIVE

Bells Beach might just be Victoria's most viewed beach, but at the same time it is one that bears few footprints. Most visitors come just to look – at the dramatic surf and the diehard surfers who brave it from dawn to dusk every day of the year.

Discovered by surfers from nearby Torquay Surf Life Saving club in the 1950s, Bells came to national attention in 1961 when the first surfing contest was held here. Today, the Bells Easter Festival is the oldest continuous professional surfing contest in the world and perhaps the most famous. In 1973, the beach from the high tide mark landward, became the world's first Surfing Recreation Reserve. The original boggy access track has made way for a new road, car parks, viewing platforms and stairs.

The surfing at Bells is consistently good because of its seabed topography and its exposure to the great wave factory of the Southern Ocean. A gently sloping limestone reef extends offshore, providing a solid platform on which the waves

BEST SURFING BEACHES

Australia is blessed with hundreds of great surfing spots. Four of the best are:

» Bells Beach, VIC – site of the world's longest running surf contest (since 1961)
» Manly, NSW – site of the first world surfing championships (1964); dedicated as Australia's first World Surfing Reserve (2012)
» Rainbow Bay–Snapper Rocks, QLD – National Surfing Reserve
» Margaret River, WA – National Surfing Reserve

Australia has rideable surf on over 3500 beaches with more than 1200 producing consistent quality board-riding waves.

BELLS BEACH

Strong Currents

High Surf

Submerged Rocks

Slippery Rocks

---

form and break, while at the shore the beach's coarse sand maintains a steep slope that creates a heavy shore break.

With its 40-metre-high golden limestone headlands, cliffs and backing bluffs, Bells has plenty of elevated viewing positions for the judges and thousands of fans who come to the Easter Festival – or for the many other visitors throughout the year. Don't stay up here, though: walk down to the beach and, if waves are low, you can cool off in the shore break. Be careful

as bigger seas create a very strong rip that flows north to neighbouring Winkipop (a beach that some argue offers better waves than Bells on its day).

Not far away is Torquay, the self-styled 'surf capital' of Australia, with its Surf World museum, the world's largest surfing museum, and a wide range of facilities. From Bells, you can follow the Great Ocean Road, one of Australia's most spectacular coastal drives, to Lorne (see Lorne) and beyond.

Home to the world's oldest continuous professional surfing contest, Bells owes its dramatic and reliable surf to the topography of its seabed and its exposure to the great wave factory of the Southern Ocean.

BONDI BEACH SYDNEY, NEW SOUTH WALES
URBAN CULTURE | INTERNATIONAL CROWD | ICEBERGS POOL | COASTAL WALK

Bondi's surf is clear and clean, if a bit boisterous at times. The infamous 'backpackers' express' current at the southern end of the beach keeps lifesavers busy fishing tourists out of the water.

Despite its sometimes-overwhelming popularity, Bondi remains a jewel, with its white curving sand, abundant surf and two protruding headlands forming an attractive semi-circular bay. Happily, the seawall and promenade were set well back leaving a 100-metre-wide beach, the widest on the east coast, that can accommodate tens of thousands of beachgoers on its well groomed sand.

The surf is clear and clean, if a bit boisterous at times thanks to the beach's orientation straight into the prevailing southerly swell. Rips are always present, including the infamous 'backpackers' express', a strong permanent current that runs out alongside the southern rocks. The heady combination of crowds and dangerous conditions means the beach is patrolled from end to end by professional lifeguards (as seen in 'Bondi Rescue') and two surf life saving clubs – including one claiming to be Australia's oldest (Manly and Bronte clubs also make this claim).

The tramway to the beach opened in 1884 but public bathing in daylight hours was prohibited until 1903. Soon after, sea bathing became so popular that concerns about public safety led to the founding of the Bondi surf life saving club in 1907. Surf patrol volunteers made their first appearance on the beach that summer.

Residential development on Bondi's vanished sand dunes and adjoining slopes began in the 1920s. The northern Ben Buckler head is packed with apartments, but the southern headland retains a slightly more natural appearance. It houses the famous Bondi Icebergs pool and clubhouse, which has the best views of any club in Sydney. From here, a coastal walk winds its way 10 kilometres south to Maroubra and, in November each year, the path is adorned with the often-quirky exhibits of the Sculpture by the Sea festival.

FIRST SURF LIFE SAVING CLUB

Informal surf life saving clubs originated in Sydney around 1903, the year after daylight bathing became legal. Among the first to be founded Australia-wide were:

» Manly, NSW – 1907
» Bondi, NSW – 1907
» Cottesloe, WA – 1909
» Tweed Heads–Coolangatta, QLD – 1911

Today there are 310 SLSCs in Australia with 161 000 active members, making this the largest national volunteer movement of its type in the world. The annual Australia Surf Life Saving Championships, with 7000 competitors, is the largest annual sporting event of its type in the world.

EARLY WHALING STATION | CONVICT-BUILT INN | NATIONAL PARK WALKS | BUSH CAMPING

Boydtown is one of the oldest settlements on the New South Wales coast but remains one of the smallest and least developed, despite its stunning location on the shores of Twofold Bay.

Wealthy London stockbroker, Benjamin Boyd, established the settlement in 1843 as a whaling station and port for his vast Monaro grazing properties. Boyd had grandiose plans but, when his colonial enterprise collapsed catastrophically, he fled to the goldfields of California where he soon disappeared.

Boydtown was abandoned, leaving only the beachfront Seahorse Inn and an unfinished church perched on a nearby ridge, both built by convict labour. For more than a century, it remained a ghost town while neighbouring Eden became the focus of regional development.

Today, the restored Seahorse Inn provides resort accommodation, while the beach that was once crossed by a jetty busy with whaling and shipping is a peaceful place to relax.

Facing east across Twofold Bay to Eden and the bay entrance, it offers gently breaking waves across a shallow sand bar. A natural foredune backs the entire beach and the only interruptions to the surrounding bushland are the inn, a large natural camping area at the southern end and a caravan park behind the centre of the beach.

At the northern end is the small Nullica River, which has supplied the sand to build the beach and shoreline 2 kilometres out into the bay. A series of low sand ridges on the way to the beach are a visible record of this process, with each ridge marking an earlier beach location. The smaller Boydtown Creek crosses the southern end of the beach next to Torarago Point and the narrow strip of sand along the base of the point makes a pleasant walk.

Boydtown is surrounded by the superb Ben Boyd National Park and many other natural attractions, including Fisheries Beach and the Light-to-Light walk via Saltwater Bay.

Historic Boydtown on the shores of Twofold Bay was once a busy port and whaling station. Surrounded by the superb Ben Boyd National Park, it is now a peaceful place to relax, walk and swim.

BRAMSTON BEACH QUEENSLAND

OUT-OF-THE-WAY LOCATION | WHISPERING CASUARINAS | CASSOWARIES | BEACH FISHING

Less than an hour's drive south of Cairns, through a spread of golden cane fields, quiet Bramston Beach is one of northern Queensland's cleanest and most picturesque beaches – as well as being the site of the state's first coconut plantation.

From the Bruce Highway, it's a winding 17-kilometre drive through the backing coastal range to reach this small, out-of-the-way community of 200 people. Most of 'town' is at the southern end of the beach: two rows of houses, two beachfront caravan parks, a solitary store, motel and the shady grass of Pacific Park, all tucked away behind a dense fringe of whispering casuarinas. Birds, wallabies, frangipanis and colourful flowers give the place a relaxed and natural feel.

You can admire the resident cassowaries but don't pat or feed them as these emu-sized birds can become aggressive if cornered. If you're after photos of beach-going cassowaries, nearby Etty Bay is also worth a visit.

The beach's 2.5-metre tide range means it is steep and deep at high tide with little surf, while low tide reveals a sloping beach and shimmering bar with low-spilling waves. The sand is made up of sediment washed down from the backing ranges, which rise to Mount Bartle Frere, the highest in Queensland at 1622 metres.

The beach fishing is great and, if you want to try your luck offshore, there is a boat ramp at the southern mangrove-lined Joyce Creek.

The small, out-of-the-way community of Bramston Beach enjoys one of the most picturesque locations in northern Queensland, less than an hour's drive from Cairns. Be warned: the resident cassowaries can be aggressive if cornered!

ANCIENT VOLCANIC LANDSCAPE | POUNDING SURF | BLOWHOLE | CAVES | LIGHTHOUSE

Dramatic Bridgewater Bay is all that remains of an ancient volcano. The southern side has been eroded by the pounding surf, opening the bay to the Southern Ocean.

Dramatic Bridgewater Bay on Victoria's wild western coast is all that remains of an ancient volcano. When the centre of the volcano collapsed, it formed a caldera, the southern side of which has been eroded by the pounding surf to open the bay to the ocean.

Today, a curving sweep of exposed beaches and rocks is bordered by Cape Bridgewater (with, at 130 metres, Victoria's highest cliffs) and Cape Nelson, both formed of volcanic basalt. The headlands are covered by massive vegetated dunes, composed of sand blown up onto the top of the cliffs by strong westerly winds over thousands of years.

Midway between Adelaide and Melbourne, this is the local surfing beach for nearby Portland, one of Victoria's oldest settlements. The main beach is at the more sheltered western end of the bay, where the Portland Surf Life Saving Club and a small cluster of houses can be found. The waves are usually lower here and break across a wide shallow sandbar, but rip currents are common so swim only when patrolled. Surfers also head here to enjoy the long spilling waves that roll into the bay.

Both capes are worth a visit. Cape Nelson with its 1884 lighthouse is a state park offering picnic areas and headland walks. The sand dunes blanketing Cape Bridgewater have been cemented into what is called 'dunerock', in places preserving a moonscape-like petrified forest. This windy site is also now home to Victoria's largest cluster of wind turbines.

Down by the rocky shore, you'll find a blowhole and a large fur-seal colony occupying a huge cave known as Parliament House.

The Great Southwest Walk runs along this section of coast taking in both capes and the beach, before continuing to Discovery Bay, all part of the Discovery Bay Coastal Park. There are campsites on both capes and in the centre of the beach.

BEACH GOLF LINKS

A true golf links is located in the sand dunes
behind the beach, where they originated on the
coast of Scotland. Some of Australia's best links
can be found at:

» Bridport, TAS – Barnbougle Golf Links
» Long Reef, NSW – Long Reef Golf Links
» Kingston, Norfolk Island – Kingston Golf Links

The bunkers on golf courses are designed to
imitate sand hollows in natural sand dunes.

BRIDPORT TASMANIA

CALM POCKET BEACHES | FORESHORE WALK | FISHING PORT | COASTAL GOLF LINKS

First settled in the 1830s, the small fishing port of Bridport in Tasmania's sparsely populated north-east is the base for the cargo vessel to nearby Flinders Island. The village nestles on granite slopes facing east across the open Anderson Bay with its back to the prevailing westerlies.

Protected from the wind, the town's five pocket beaches – Old Pier, Mattingley, Croquet Lawn, Eastmans and Goftons – are mostly less than 100 metres long and bordered by beautiful rounded granite boulders. Waves are usually low to calm, with a shallow bar extending out to sea. It's so shallow here that the old jetty had to run out 500 metres before it could find deep water.

All of the beaches offer sheltered, safe swimming and are easily accessible by car, or on foot via the delightful 2-kilometre easy walking track that runs from town through the shady sloping foreshore reserve to the Granite Point Coastal Reserve in the north.

Bridport offers sea, lake and river fishing, sheltered beaches backed by shady picnic areas, a sailing club at Croquet Lawn Beach, a beachfront caravan park in the reserve and one of the world's best golf links courses. The 80-hectare Barnbougle Dunes Golf Links makes creative use of the undulating dunes, like some of Ireland and Scotland's wild coastal golf links.

Bridport's five pocket beaches are mostly less than 100 metres long and are linked by a delightful 2-kilometre walking track through the shady foreshore reserve. The historic fishing village fronts the sheltered waters of Anderson Bay, making it an ideal family destination. Golfers can enjoy the superb Barnbougle links set among the coastal dunes.

Welcome to

DENDY STREET BEACH
Brighton, Victoria

home of the
BRIGHTON BATHING BOXES

Your active support is sought to protect
the foreshore environment, including
dunes, vegetation, marine life and
the bathing boxes.

Bathing box security; transfer and
other matters may be referred to the
Committee of Management.

BRIGHTON BATHING BOX ASSOCIATION INC.
PO Box 230, Brighton, Victoria, 3186
Telephone 9591 0505

brighton bathing box association inc.

BRIGHTON BEACH MELBOURNE, VICTORIA

COLOURFUL BEACH BOXES | CALM WATERS | CITY LIFESTYLE CLOSE TO MELBOURNE'S CBD

Brighton Beach is Australia's only art gallery on the high tide mark, thanks to its colourful array of 82 privately owned beach changing rooms, known locally as beach boxes. The colours of the boxes are constantly changing as the light shifts – or when creative owners get busy with paintbrushes and palettes.

The boxes evolved from the wheeled 'bathing machines' used in Victorian England to preserve modesty. Queen Victoria installed one at Osbourne House on the Isle of Wight in the 1840s and, by the 1860s, Melburnians were following suit on the shores of Port Phillip Bay.

Sadly, local councils ordered the removal of many boxes from neighbouring beaches in the 1960s, but Brighton's survived long enough for their heritage value to be recognised. Today, they can fetch high prices on the rare occasions they come on the market but, while the boxes are licensed, the beach is free to all, like every Australian beach.

The beach here has been patrolled by a lifesaving club since 1923 and is readily accessible from the lifesaving club car park or, if you park on the street, you can walk through the vegetated foreshore reserve located between the road and the beach.

You will find usually low waves at the shore breaking across a shallow sand bar. Brighton is only one of the many calm beaches of Port Phillip Bay, which extend to within 2 kilometres of the CBD, giving Melbourne more 'city beaches' than any other Australian city.

Port Melbourne, St Kilda, Elwood and Brighton all have lifesaving clubs on beaches that have been a major recreational outlet for more than a century.

Brighton's colourful beach boxes are a legacy of the 19th-century drive to preserve modesty on the beach. These days, owners use the boxes to display their artistic talents, making this beach an art gallery on the high tide mark.

BRITISH ADMIRAL BEACH
KING ISLAND, TASMANIA

SHIPWRECKS | KELP COLLECTORS | SURFING | WIND-SWEPT DUNES | OCEAN SUNSETS

Dotted along the rough, reef-strewn west coast of King Island are monuments to ships wrecked in its wild Bass Strait seas and to the unfortunate sailors who perished as a result. More than 800 lives were lost here during the 19th century and local kangaroo hunters and sealers often buried the bodies in unmarked graves in the sand dunes.

In 1874, the *British Admiral* was an iron clipper bringing new settlers to the Australian colonies when it was wrecked on a reef off the beach that now bears its name. Seventy-nine people died, making it the island's third worst shipwreck.

Fortunately, getting here is a bit easier these days, as the island is just a short flight from Devonport or Melbourne.

British Admiral Beach is the best known of King Island's 45 beaches and offers the best surf – though for experienced surfers only, as waves are usually boisterous and strong rip currents and reefs litter the surf zone.

Just 2 kilometres south of the island's main town and harbour, Currie (home to almost half the island's 1700 residents), the beach is also great for a brisk walk, with pounding waves on one side and wind-swept dunes on the other. You can watch the sun set over the ocean here and you're likely to encounter local fishers. After a storm, the kelp collectors will be out, with their interesting range of vehicles, hauling kelp off the beach to dry in the racks at Currie, before being exported internationally.

King Island's British Admiral beach is named for the iron clipper wrecked in its wild Bass Strait waters in 1874, with the loss of 79 lives. The waves here are for experienced surfers only as the sea is littered with reefs and strong rip currents.

SHIPWRECKS

Many ships have been wrecked around Australia's coastline. Among the most famous were:

» *Batavia* (1629) – Houtman Abrolhos, WA
» *Zuytdorp* (1712) – Zuytdorp Cliffs, WA
» *Endeavour* (1770) – Endeavour Reef, QLD
» *Sydney Cove* (1797) – Preservation Island, TAS
» *Cataraqui* (1845) – King Island, Bass Strait
» *British Admiral* (1874) – King Island, Bass Strait
» *Loch Ard* (1878) – Shipwreck coast, VIC

Each of these wrecks, far from home and assistance, has a fascinating story – some heroic, many tragic. Only *Endeavour* survived to sail again.

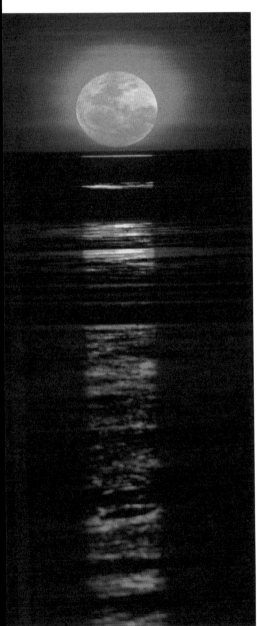

CABLE BEACH BROOME, WESTERN AUSTRALIA

PEARLING | MULTICULTURAL HISTORY | STAIRWAY TO THE MOON | BIG TIDES

Broome is an exotic mix of red-dirt outback and white-sand beaches, of cattle and pearls, and of Aboriginal, Asian and European heritage. It offers everything from 5-star cuisine, to indigenous art galleries, pearl emporiums, an historic open-air cinema, funky shops and a great weekend market.

Cable is this historic Kimberley pearling town's beach, extending south from the northern access point down to Gantheaume Point, famous for its fossilised dinosaur footprints. Pearling luggers still shelter here in the lee of the point.

Although tourists have discovered Broome in recent years, the beach remains in a relatively pristine state, still backed by natural sand dunes. It's busiest at the northern end where the once rustic old camping area has been replaced by upmarket resorts and dwellings, alongside a selection of camping and hostel accommodation, a crocodile park, hotel and surf life saving club.

The beach is famous for its gargantuan tides, reaching up to 10 metres, which are amplified by the broad, shallow continental shelf along this part of the Indian Ocean coast. In just a few hours, the outgoing tide can widen the beach from 10 to 400 metres. Watch where you leave your towel if you go for a wander at low tide, as the returning tide comes in very fast indeed.

The beach offers lots of activities including camel rides, paddle boarding, parasailing and four-wheel driving. It is usually calm, though there can be the occasional wave for surfing. There's a long 'clothing optional' beach round the low boulders at the northern end.

Visit Broome at full moon, to see the famous 'stairway to the moon' phenomenon when moonlight spills across the ridged sand flats of Roebuck Bay.

BIGGEST TIDES

The highest tidal range in Australia ranks third in the world. Here are the four highest:

» Derby, WA – 11.8 m
» Broome, WA – 9.8 m
» Wyndham, WA – 8.4 m
» Broad Sound, QLD – 8 m

The smallest tidal range in Australia is just 0.4 m at WA's Windy Harbour. And the Gulf of Carpentaria at times has only one low and one high tide each day.

The historic pearling town of Broome offers a vibrant multicultural history and dramatic landscape with some of Australia's biggest tides. Visit at full moon to see the famous 'stairway to the moon', when moonlight spills across the ridged sand flats of Roebuck Bay.

CAPE HILLSBOROUGH QUEENSLAND

CORAL SEA VIEWS | NATIONAL PARK WALKS | WATERFALLS | SUNBAKING KANGAROOS

The forested slopes of the rugged Cape Hillsborough National Park are home to creeks, valleys, caves, waterfalls and a rich tropical ecosystem. Sunbaking kangaroos are unfazed by humans.

On this wide, gently sloping beach fronting the Coral Sea, you'll often find sunbaking kangaroos unfazed by humans – and a host of other wildlife on land and in the sea.

The forested slopes of the rugged Cape Hillsborough National Park are home to creeks, valleys, caves, waterfalls and a rich tropical ecosystem. The mix of rainforest and eucalyptus forest creates a birdwatcher's mecca, with over 170 species of birds recorded in the small park – not to mention 28 tropical butterflies, 32 mammals, 10 frogs, 27 reptiles and more than 500 plants. The adjoining marine park is equally rich in wildlife, including the bubbler crab, which leaves intricate patterns on the beach, and many different sea creatures in the tidal pools. The cape's volcanic origins are evident in the local thunder eggs, small spherical rocks containing a crystal-rich chamber.

The beach is on the north-eastern side of the low sandy isthmus that links the prominent cape to the mainland. Sheltered by the cape and inshore islands, it usually offers low-spilling waves and light winds. If the solar intensity becomes too strong, there's a large shady picnic park in the trees behind.

The cape has five great walks: a boardwalk though the mangrove and melaleuca forest highlighting indigenous coastal life, a beach walk to neighbouring Beachcomber Cove where a waterfall cascades though tropical rainforest onto the beach (bringing so much fresh water that at times it turns the surf zone fresh), the Yuibera Plant Trail via Hidden Valley which highlights indigenous bush food, a low-tide walk to Wedge Island with its soft corals, and – best of them all – the Andrews Point track with its five spectacular lookouts offering views of the beach through the native hoop pines.

Cape Hillsborough is only 50 kilometres from Mackay so if you're short of time it makes a great day trip.

CAPE LEVEQUE
DAMPIER PENINSULA, WESTERN AUSTRALIA

RED SANDSTONE | WHITE DUNES | REMOTE LOCATION | BIG TIDES | SPECTACULAR SUNSETS

This is one for the adventurous. Cape Leveque lies near the northern tip of the Dampier Peninsula, a 220-kilometre, 3-hour haul on a red corrugated dirt road from Broome (although there is also a landing strip for light planes). And the road in is the only road out.

When you get there though, you will find one of nature's wonders. The rich red sandstone cape is surrounded by the equally bright red pindan plains, all capped by pure white sand dunes and leafy pandanus trees, the two in places intermingling to form shades of pink. The sunrises and sunsets are spectacular.

On either side of the cape are brilliant clear waters and white beaches made of almost pure silica. The most popular is the crescent of sand on the eastern side, with its backing of pure white sand dunes. The biggest tides in Australia mean the shoreline here is always changing, and the beaches on the western side are submerged at high tide.

The cape is located on Bardi land and the nearby Djarindjin and One Arm Point Aboriginal communities operate an award-winning resort, a laid-back tropical wilderness safari camp that offers everything from camping to cabins with a touch of luxury.

There's a lot to do here: swimming in the warm waters, beachcombing for colourful shells, reef walking, whale and bird watching, hunting and eating mud crabs, fishing from the beach or by boat, 4WD tours along the beaches or aerial tours of the rugged Kimberley coast and islands. The historic pearl inlay church at nearby Beagle Bay is also worth a visit.

The rich red sandstone of Cape Leveque is surrounded by bright red pindan plains capped by pure white sand dunes and leafy pandanus trees. It's worth the three-hour haul on a corrugated dirt road from Broome, if only for the spectacular sunrises and sunsets.

The white sands of Cape Peron sit below bright red pindan bluffs in the Shark Bay World Heritage Area. The biggest area of seagrass meadows in Australia is home to the country's largest dugong population.

CAPE PERON SHARK BAY, WESTERN AUSTRALIA

WORLD HERITAGE AREA | SEAGRASS MEADOWS | DUGONGS | WILDERNESS CAMPING

Shark Bay on the desert coast of Western Australia is actually more famous for its dugongs and dolphins than for sharks. This was one of the first areas of the Australian coast to be explored by Europeans. It's the site of Dutch navigator Dirk Hartog's historic landing in 1616, and the bay was named by English buccaneer William Dampier in 1699 and mapped by the French explorer, Nicolas Baudin, in 1802.

The Shark Bay World Heritage Area is still largely pristine and includes 13 national and marine parks as well as Monkey Mia where people come to see the dolphins. The irregularly shaped shoreline extends over 900 kilometres and has 240 mostly long and low-energy beaches separated by steep bluffs. These front the largest area of seagrass meadows in Australia, which is home to the country's largest dugong population.

So much evaporation occurs over the bay that the salinity at the southern end is twice that of normal sea water, allowing ancient stromalites to grow in Hamelin Pool along with the salt-tolerant molluscs that have produced Shell Beach (see Shell Beach).

The best of the beaches sits at the very tip of the central Peron Peninsula, at Cape Peron in the Francis Peron National Park (Peron was the naturalist on Baudin's expedition). It's worth the 50-kilometre drive from Denham, much of it on dusty red tracks, to visit the small cape beach, with its white sands, perched below bright red pindan bluffs. You can view and photograph both this and the longer beaches on either side from the top of the bluffs, or walk down and swim in the crystal-clear waters where seagrass meadows extend to the tip of the cape.

The Peron Peninsula is also home to Project Eden, which is attempting to rid it of feral animals and provide a safe haven for native animals. Basic camping is available nearby at Bottle Bay, Gregories and Herald Bight.

CASUARINA BEACH
DARWIN, NORTHERN TERRITORY

CITY BEACH | TROPICAL FOREST | WILDLIFE | WALKING TRACKS | CROCODILES

Casuarina Beach is Darwin's favourite coastal playground. This wide sandy beach with its shady casuarinas faces north-east into the Timor Sea, turning its back to the prevailing trade winds. Just 10 kilometres north of the city centre, the beach curves from the slippery claystone bluffs at Dripstone Cliffs to the sandy tip of Lee Point, Darwin's northern boundary.

Casuarina is the longest of the 12 beaches on Darwin's irregular northern shoreline. The beach, dunes and central Sandy Creek are part of the Casuarina Coastal Reserve, which features mangroves, monsoon vine-forest and casuarina woodlands, as well the biggest range of wildlife in the Darwin area. The only development is the Darwin Surf Life Saving Club at the southern end and three parking and picnic areas.

The 7-metre tide range produces a beach that expands from 50 metres wide at high tide to more than 200 metres at low tide, revealing in the process a couple of undulating intertidal ridges and runnels. The beach is usually calm and, as well as swimming and fishing, offers walking and cycling tracks, and a dog exercise and horse riding area in the park behind. There is a clothing optional area north of the Dariba Road picnic area.

Lurking crocodiles are removed from Darwin beaches, but visitors should be aware that they could appear at any time, particularly during the summer, as can the deadly box jellyfish or painful 'stingers'.

Casuarina is the longest of the 12 beaches on Darwin's irregular northern shoreline. The coastal reserve features mangroves, monsoon vine-forest and casuarina woodlands, as well as the biggest range of wildlife in the Darwin area.

CATHERINE HILL BAY NEW SOUTH WALES

HISTORIC COAL MINING VILLAGE | PRISTINE BEACH | SURFING | MOVIE HISTORY

Heritage-listed Catherine Hill Bay is the only surviving example of an historic coastal coal-mining settlement and port in Australia, all set around a beautiful undeveloped beach. In fact, the beach owes its preservation to the coal mine, which has controlled and limited development for 150 years.

Settlement began here in 1865 and the first shipment of coal left here in 1873. The bay was named after the schooner *Catherine Hill*, which was wrecked in the bay in 1867.

Located just off the old Pacific Highway about 100 kilometres north of Sydney, Catherine Hill Bay is signposted only on the northern approaches and the only access is via 'private' company roads. As you arrive from the south, you pass piles of coal from the still-working mine to reach a small weatherboard village – a company town with old company houses that turn their backs on the beach views behind.

There is also one pub, although once there were dozens for the thousands of miners who worked here.

Until 1963, a railway line ran along the back of the beach delivering coal to the southern jetty, where '60 miler' coal steamers carried it to Sydney. The decommissioned jetty is still there, but otherwise the beach remains in a pretty natural state, apart from the surf life saving club established by the coal miners in 1928. Wallarah National Park lies just to the north and Munmorah State Conservation Area borders the southern end adding to the natural feel. Both contain more beaches and headlands to explore.

The beach, also known as Middle Camp, is fairly exposed and renowned for its surf and beach breaks, which have long attracted surfers from Newcastle and Sydney. In 1977, actor Mel Gibson made his film debut here in *Summer City* – billed as a 'sizzling, sexy surf epic'.

Only 100 kilometres from Sydney, pristine Catherine Hill Bay owes it preservation to the coal mine, which has controlled and limited development here for 150 years. The mine's decommissioned jetty still stands but otherwise the beach remains in a pretty natural state.

COSY CORNER BAY OF FIRES, TASMANIA

GRANITE BOULDERS | ORANGE LICHEN | CLEAR WATERS | COASTAL WALKS | BUSH CAMPING

The Bay of Fires was named by British navigator Tobias Furneaux because of the many Aboriginal fires he saw here when he sailed past in 1773.

The Bay of Fires Conservation Area is renowned for its coastal walks and its 40 beaches, half of them small pockets of sand less than 100 metres long and all bounded by rocks or low headlands of massive granite covered with orange lichen. In places, these have been eroded into great clusters of large rounded boulders, including the set known as Old Man Rocks.

The stunning natural beaches along the open 35-kilometre-long bay include Policemans, Pebbly, Jacks Lookout, Break Yoke, The Gardens, Swimcart, Matey, Suicide, Honeymoon, Beerbarrel and Binalong Bay, but the best of the lot is Cosy Corner. This 500-metre-long gem

has the pure white quartz sand typical of this coast, sloping into clear aqua waters. Its usually low swell breaks across a series of bars and rip channels so be cautious swimming even if it looks calm. Surfers will discover more breaks in these parts, although it can be fickle.

Cosy Corner has several free and shady campsites, but you'll need to bring everything with you, as the only facilities are an amenities block. Free camping is also available at Sloop Reef, Seaton Cove, Swimcart and Jeanneret beaches and on the shores of Big Lagoon.

The Bay of Fires is accessible in the north from Anson Bay and in the south via St Helens– Binalong Bay. The 10-kilometre drive north from Binalong passes 15 beaches, including spectacular Taylors Beach and Cosy Corner, before ending at The Gardens.

The Bay of Fires is renowned for coastal walks around its 40 beaches, many of them pockets of sand less than 100 metres long. With its pure white sand and clear aqua waters, Cosy Corner is the pick of the lot.

COTTESLOE
PERTH, WESTERN AUSTRALIA

URBAN LIFESTYLE | PEOPLE WATCHING | INDIAN
OCEAN SUNSETS | GENTLE WAVES | WA'S FIRST
SURF LIFE SAVING CLUB

Cottesloe has long been Perth's favourite ocean beach: beach lovers have been coming here in droves since the opening of the Cottesloe railway station in 1880. Western Australia's first surf life saving club was established here in 1909 and the second a few hundred metres up the beach at North Cottesloe in 1912.

Like all Perth beaches, Cottesloe is partly sheltered from large swell by Rottnest Island, resulting in usually low waves that create a narrow, gentle surf zone and make the beach popular with swimmers who do laps of the beach. The steady stream of beachgoers from dawn to dusk includes wealthy Perth fashionistas, salty locals and sunburnt backpackers. The usually wide beach offers volleyball nets, thatched shelters and enough room for big crowds on hot summer days and evenings, when many stay to watch the sun set over the Indian Ocean.

The rock groyne at the southern end is a popular fishing hang-out and a little further south a surfing reef off the Cable Station bluffs is popular with stand-up paddle boarders.

If Cottesloe is crowded, there are plenty more options to the north, where the city beaches stretch another 12 kilometres to Scarborough and Triggs, including a clothing optional 3-kilometre section between Swanbourne and City Beach.

The citizens of Perth have been flocking to Cottesloe in droves since the railway reached here in 1880. Like all Perth beaches, it is partly sheltered by Rottnest Island, meaning waves are mostly gentle and family-friendly.

CRESCENT HEAD NEW SOUTH WALES

LONG WAVES | CREEK SWIMMING | QUIET CHARM | OCEAN-FRONT GOLF | NATIONAL PARKS

Crescent Head retains its quiet, out of the way charm, despite having been a surfing mecca ever since its long, easy waves were discovered by surfers in the 1960s. Its classic peeling right-hand break attracts surfers, particularly long-boarders, all year round and when the surf is running the beachfront car park is packed with them. The beach was proclaimed a National Surfing Reserve in 2008.

Before its discovery by surfers, this was the beach for the inland town of Kempsey – the Kempsey–Crescent Head Surf Life Saving Club was established here in 1921 when a timber track made its way through the boggy swamps to reach the beach.

The beach is dominated by the grassy headland after which the place is named, and an ocean-front six-hole golf course extends up to the higher, adjoining head. From the crest of the headland, look south to wild and rocky Pebbly Beach (the most dangerous in New South Wales) and north along the lines of the peeling waves, most with a surfer on board, to the mouth of Killick Creek. The creek marks the start of Killick Beach, which extends for 15 kilometres up to Hungry Head and Hat Head National Park.

A footbridge across the shallow Killick Creek links the beach to the park and caravan park. The surf club patrols the southern end of the beach and the creek mouth, both of which are very popular with swimmers and all sorts of floating devices. There is also a boat ramp for fishers who want to wind their way out through the surf.

Crescent offers a range of restaurants and is a great base for exploring by 4WD (with a permit) Killick Beach and the national park to the north, or down the gravel road south to Point Plomer and all the pristine beaches and headlands in between.

Its classic right-hand peeling break has made Crescent Head a favourite surfing destination for decades, but this charming, out-of-the-way town in northern NSW also offers safe family swimming in shallow Killick Creek.

Crescent Head **National Surfing Reserve**

Crescent Head was the first stop
for surfers heading north from Sydney in
pursuit of the perfect wave. Since the 1960's, surfers
have been attracted to this area to experience the quality
of the wave and the unique natural environment. The coastal
beauty and pristine beaches of Crescent Head continue to attract
surfers and visitors from throughout Australia and overseas.

Crescent Head, traditional country of the Dunghutti people, is home to osprey,
sea eagles, pelicans, dolphins and migrating whales.

National Surfing Reserves recognise sites of cultural and historical significance in
Australian surfing. They acknowledge the surfing way of life and link past,
present and future generations with our oceans, waves and coastline.

The Crescent Head Community asks you to
Share • Respect • Preserve

Hon Tony Kelly MP   Brad Farmer   Cr Betty Green
NSW Minister   National Surfing   Mayor Kempsey Shire
for Lands   Reserves   Council

Dedicated on 14th June 2008

dhalkungga yalanggur biramay

CYLINDERS BEACH
NORTH STRADBROKE ISLAND, QUEENSLAND

ISLAND BEACH | FERRY RIDE FROM BRISBANE | BIG SAND DUNES | SURF

North Stradbroke Island, a short ferry ride from Brisbane, is the world's second largest sand island. The pick of its 14 beaches is Cylinders, which offers the best surf on the island as well as some shelter from prevailing winds.

Think sand and lots of it. You'll be shaking it off for weeks after you visit – after all, this island is made of it. North 'Straddie's' bush, lakes, surf and big sand dunes make it one of the best and most affordable island destinations in Australia – all just a ferry ride from Brisbane.

North Stradbroke Island is a massive elongated accumulation of sand, 40 kilometres due east of the Queensland capital. It's the world's second largest sand island, after Fraser Island to the north (see Seventy Five Mile Beach). North Stradbroke lost its 21-kilometre-long tail, which became South Stradbroke Island when the island was split in two by a violent storm in 1896. Today, the island has a population of 2000 mostly located in the three small settlements of Dunwich, Amity and Point Lookout. The original inhabitants, the indigenous Quandamooka people are also well represented, particularly in the historic Dunwich area.

The island is 35 kilometres long and surrounded by 14 beaches but the pick of them is the 500-metre-long north-facing Cylinders, round the corner from Point Lookout at the north-eastern tip of the island. It has some shelter from waves and wind, and the waves that wrap round the point create the best surf on the island. The beach was named for the waves' cylindrical shape.

Waves are lower at the shore, but be careful if they are higher than 1 metre as a current can run down the beach. Sand pulses periodically move round the head producing quality surf and sometimes enclosing a shallow lagoon when they near the shore. The beach has a large car park, shady foreshore reserve, including a picnic and camping area, and is patrolled by lifeguards over summer.

Ferries, both fast and slow, arrive from Cleveland on the mainland every hour, and a good road network connects the three island communities. Four-wheel drive vehicles can be driven on the bush tracks and (with a permit) on the beach, which can be soft and hazardous.

DIGGERS BEACH NEW SOUTH WALES

HORSESHOE-SHAPED BAY | UNCROWDED BEACH | NATURAL HEADLANDS | QUIET LOCATION

The Coffs Harbour coast features a series of small headland-bound beaches, some of which, like Diggers, are backed by valleys containing small communities or resorts. Set in a beautiful horseshoe-shaped bay, Diggers is made up of two strips of sand totalling just 1 kilometre in length. The beach lies between two prominent and undeveloped headlands that stretch about 300 metres out to sea.

A low-key resort straddles the small Jordans Creek, which drains out across the northern end of the beach. Public access is at the southern Diggers Beach Reserve, which offers a car park, playground, barbecues, picnic shelters, two viewing platforms and beach showers. The beach is rarely crowded as it is off the main road and can be hard to find.

The main beach curves round in the shelter of the southern rocks and surf usually breaks across the bar, making it a popular surfing beach and the site of year-round surf schools. Be careful where you swim, as rip currents are usually present. Lifeguards patrol the beach during summer.

The northern beach, Little Diggers, has densely vegetated slopes rising behind and is reached by a short walk round the rocks. It is an unofficial clothing optional beach, so be prepared. It receives slightly higher waves and can have a strong rip running out by the rocks, so is less suitable for swimming.

Charming Diggers Beach on the Coffs Harbour coast is made up of two strips of sand totalling just 1 kilometre in length. The beach is rarely crowded as it is off the main road and can be hard to find.

DUNBOGAN—DIAMOND HEAD
NEW SOUTH WALES

NATIONAL PARK | WILDERNESS WALKS | BIRD LIFE | KANGAROOS | LITERARY HISTORY

Dunbogan Beach in Crowdy Head National Park offers a stunning array of landscapes and wildlife experiences, from the large quartz crystals that sparkle in the sun in the volcanic rock formations of Diamond Head, to coastal wetlands with their abundant bird life.

Magnificent Crowdy Head National Park, just south of the twin towns of Camden Haven–Laurieton near Port Macquarie, borders 20 kilometres of coastline with four long sweeping beaches. The pick of the bunch is Dunbogan Beach, which curves away to the south between Camden and Diamond heads. Its clean white sand slopes in a gentle gradient, creating a wide surf zone with an outer bar where waves break during bigger seas. In the hinterland, North Brother Mountain rises to 500 metres creating an imposing backdrop.

When exploring this great stretch of beach, start at the northern lookout on Camden Head for a spectacular view down the coast, then head south stopping for a picnic or a dip at one of the three national park picnic areas along the way. At the southern end, Diamond Head Camping Area provides a grassy camping spot complete with friendly resident kangaroos.

The headland at Diamond Head is composed of Triassic volcanic trachyte, which has a rich reddish colour and forms steep, jagged gullies along the eastern face. Navigator and explorer James Cook named this headland 'Indian Head' in 1770 when he sighted 'natives' on its slope. The present name derives from the large quartz crystals that sparkle in the sun.

A loop walking track on Diamond Head gives sweeping views of the beaches in both directions. The return inland track passes through a fern glade, pockets of coastal rainforest and stands of the uniquely Australian grass tree. Here, and in the extensive wetlands and coastal heath elsewhere in the park, the native plants attract a wide variety of bird life. The beach to the south of the headland and the track itself are named after the poet, writer and early coastal activist, Kylie Tennant, whose historic slab hut has been restored in the Kylie Hut walk-in camping area, located behind the northern end of the beach.

Dunbogan Beach is usually sheltered in the southern corner but rip channels and currents dominate the remainder of the beach, so beware if you choose to swim in the unpatrolled surf.

EAST WOODY BEACH
ARNHEM LAND, NORTHERN TERRITORY

REMOTE BEACH | INDIGENOUS CULTURE | WETLANDS | FISHING | SURFING | CROCODILES

This is not the kind of beach to just swing by for a dip, as it's a 1100 kilometre drive from Darwin and 730 kilometres from the highway to Nhulunbuy (Gove) in eastern Arnhem Land - most of it on the dirt Central Arnhem Land road. Once there you will find the port of Gove located at the western end of the Gove Peninsula, which is lined by long sandy tropical beaches.

The pick of the beaches is East Woody, located on the north-east shore of the peninsula. It begins at East Woody Island a 25-metre-high mound of rounded granite boulders that is usually tied to the beach by a low sandy spit, and backed by a mangrove-lined creek. The beach then extends to the east for 3.5 kilometres to Cape Wirrawawoi. the northern tip of the peninsula.

East Woody forms the northern boundary of the township and is easily reached via the golf course road, with an access road paralleling the beach leading to three beach access areas, the western one ending at the creek mouth. A band of low dunes fringed by shady casuarina trees backs the entire beach. The beach faces north, with the trade winds usually blowing offshore producing relative calm conditions and crystal clear water. At high tide the water is deep against the beach, shoaling as the tide falls.

Waves are usually low so the hazards on this beach are mainly biological, including stingers, the occasional passing crocodile and even water

buffalo. The Gove Surf Life Saving Club has a lifeguarding crocodile as its club emblem.

Sometimes when the 'surf' is up, there are waves to be had at Little Bondi or Wirruwuy beach, both located on the more exposed Arnhem Peninsula 20 kilometres to the south-east. Wirruwuy is the site of Australia's first indigenous surf club.

One of the most remote beaches in Australia, East Woody near the bauxite-mining town of Nhulunbuy in eastern Arnhem Land is a 1100-kilometre drive from Darwin. The area is a stronghold of indigenous culture so you can enjoy cultural tours and interpretative walking trails.

ECO BEACH KIMBERLEY, WESTERN AUSTRALIA

REMOTE LOCATION | BIG TIDES | SEA KAYAKING | WHALES | FISHING | ROCK FORMATIONS

On Australia's remote north-west coast, Eco Beach lies on the southern side of Roebuck Bay some 40 kilometres south of Broome. From Cape Villaret in the south, the beach winds its way northwards for 12 kilometres to the tip of a low sandy spit where Jacks Creek enters the sea.

This beach typifies the north-west, with plenty of sand backed by grassy dunes that extend a few hundred metres inland. The usually calm conditions or low waves make this a wonderful place to enjoy the warm aqua-blue waters of the Indian Ocean. But also typical of the north-west are the big tides – up to 10 metres. Do check the tide charts, as what may be a narrow beach at high tide could extend for hundreds of metres at low tide.

Although it is remote and largely undeveloped, this section of coast is home to an eco resort, which nestles quietly in the dunes in the lee of the magnificent curving stretch of white sand. This is a popular choice for those who prefer not to rough it when camping.

There is plenty to do here. The beach is a base for sea kayaking, whale watching and beach fishing. Or, if you want to try creek fishing, you could take a 4WD up to Jacks Creek where you might catch, among others, barramundi, threadfin or mangrove jack. Those who want to stretch their legs might want to walk south along the beach towards dune-capped Cape Villaret where, along the way, there are many interesting and colourful rock formations, caves and layered bluffs and some secluded pockets of sand that are swept clean with each high tide.

Remote Eco Beach offers a classic Kimberley seascape, with its sandy dunes, clear waters and big tides. Visitors can wander along the beach to admire the colourful rock formations and caves or try their luck fishing in nearby Jacks Creek.

LONGEST BEACHES

Australia has four very long beaches. They are:

» Eighty Mile Beach, WA – 220 km
» The Coorong, SA – 194 km
» Ninety Mile Beach, VIC – 127 km
» Seventy Five Mile, QLD – 89 km

The other states have no beaches longer than 26 km. The average length of all 11 761 Australian beaches is just 1.4 km.

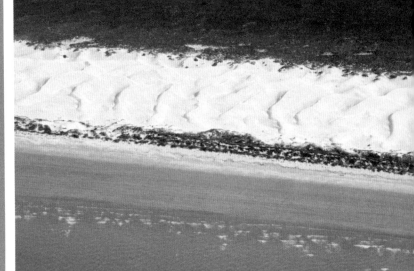

EIGHTY MILE BEACH WESTERN AUSTRALIA

Eighty Mile Beach, in the remote, arid north-west of Western Australia, is actually longer than its names suggests: at 220 kilometres, it is one of the three longest beaches in Australia. Facing north-west, it curves in a gentle arc between Cape Keraudren in the south and Cape Missiessy at the northern end. The French maritime explorer Nicolas Baudin named both capes when he explored this coast in 1801.

The fine carbonate sand found here is a by-product of the massive shell population that lives on the seabed in the clear ocean waters off the beach. When these organisms die their shells, in myriad shapes, colours and sizes are washed up onto the beach, where they accumulate by the tens of thousands. But the shells are just one reason the beach has become world renowned – the other is the shorebirds. Each year an astonishing half a million migratory shorebirds descend on Eighty Mile Beach, flying in from their feeding and breeding grounds in the Arctic Circle. Red knots, bar-tailed godwits, curlew sandpipers, red-necked stints and many more species migrate here during the northern winter.

Eighty Mile Beach is almost halfway between Port Hedland and Broome, so it's a long way from anywhere. Only two public roads run out to the coast from the Northwest Highway, one at Cape Keraudren and the other midway along the beach at Wallal. Both sites are very popular with campers, particularly during the balmy winter months. However it's at Wallal that most come to collect shells, fish, walk, drive and swim.

This is also a great place to see the dramatic changes, typical of this coast, between high and low tides when the beach may widen from 50 to 1000 metres. If you do follow the tide out be prepared to be literally chased as it comes back in; it moves across the flats at an incredible 3 metres per minute. Small sharks also follow the tide in, so it's wise to take care.

Australia's longest beach, Eighty Mile in the arid north-west of Western Australia also boasts the nation's finest array of shells, thanks to the huge population of shell creatures living in its clear waters. An astonishing half a million migratory shorebirds descend on the beach each year during the summer months.

EIMEO MACKAY, QUEENSLAND

CORAL SEA WATERS | BEACH PUB WITH VIEWS | MANGROVE-LINED CREEK | BEACH WALKS

Eimeo is tucked away at the head of its own small peninsula not far from the central Queensland town of Mackay. Its Pacific Hotel may have a claim to the best pub views in Australia.

Eimeo beach is a little gem. Tucked away at the head of its own small peninsula just outside the central Queensland town of Mackay, it is linked to the mainland by mango-lined Mango Avenue.

On the western side of the peninsula is the aptly named Sunset Bay. A small tidal creek and tidal shoals occupy the eastern end of the beach where low Dolphin Point extends seawards. The Eimeo Surf Life Saving Club is located at the base of the point and lifesavers patrol the beach during summer.

The Mackay region has a 5-metre tidal range, which means that at high tide Eimeo is a narrow beach dropping into deep water. As the tide recedes it reveals the steep high-tide beach with a 100-metre-wide shallow beach at its base, which widens in the south to form extensive tidal shoals off the creek mouth. Mangroves line the creek behind the beach. At low tide, you can walk from Eimeo Beach to neighbouring Dolphin Point and, if you're lucky, you can even catch a wave off the point during bigger seas.

Eimeo Point, which forms the western boundary of the beach, is the site of Eimeo's other key attraction – the Pacific Hotel. Australia has many beachside pubs that boast great ocean views but this one has entered into folklore as the pub with one of the best views on the Australian coast. At this unique rest stop perched 60 metres above the beach you can fill your lungs with pure Coral Sea air while you gaze out over the vast Pacific Ocean and at Brampton, Keswick and St Bees islands. The pub started life as a hunting lodge built by a former seafarer, Captain Armitage, in the late 1880s when guests arrived from Mackay by boat. Armitage named the site because it reminded him of Eimeo in Tahiti (pronounced Ay-ee-may-oh).

BEST BEACHFRONT PUBS

If you want a location where there is a great view of the
beach from the local pub try these:

» Eimeo, QLD – Eimeo Pacific Hotel
» Yamba, NSW – Pacific Hotel
» Lorne, VIC – Grand Pacific Hotel
» Cottesloe, WA – Cottesloe Beach Hotel
» Karumba, QLD – End of the Road Motel

At Cottesloe and Karumba there is the bonus of
stunning sunsets.

ELEPHANT ROCKS WESTERN AUSTRALIA

NATIONAL PARK | ROCK POOLS | SNORKELLING | WALKS | WILDFLOWERS | WEATHERED ROCKS

Small but beautiful, William Bay National Park covers an 11-kilometre-long section of coast just west of Denmark in southern Western Australia. Its spectacular beaches, coves and pools are all bordered and sheltered by massive granite headlands, weathered boulders and reefs, which bear the brunt of the heavy seas.

The best way to experience the park is to start from the Greens Pool car park and explore on foot the kilometre of coast to either side.

The main Greens Pool beach area begins just below the car park and extends to the west for 750 metres, sheltered along its length by a series of semi-submerged granite rocks and reefs. This is a very popular spot, so if you want to avoid the crowds follow the walking track east. This leads you first to Elephant Rocks Beach where two giant elephant-sized rocks dominate the centre of the beach. More huge rocks sit at the entrance to a narrow cove

that extends inland for 200 metres. Backed by granite all round, and with several large 'elephants' bathing in its waters, the cove has a sandy beach and seafloor.

Next is the 50-metre-long Smooth Pool beach set in a V in the granite and completely sheltered by massive granite reefs extending a few hundred metres offshore. For a longer walk, continue east to Madfish Bay where at low tide a tombolo connects an elongated granite islet to the shore. Around the next corner is Waterfall Beach, which is also accessible by car.

This stretch of coast is a delightful place to explore, fish, snorkel or simply enjoy one of the most scenic natural swimming locations in Australia. Inshore, the waters are usually calm and pool-like; the bigger Southern Ocean waves break offshore on the rocks and reefs. In spring the wildflowers are superb and the scenery, with its ever-changing moods, is stunning year-round.

The smooth granite boulders of the William Bay National Park, in southern Western Australia, look like giant elephants bathing in the protected waters. The sheltering rocks make this a calm place to swim or snorkel.

BEST BEACH CEMETERY

If you want to rest in peace by the beach you should book
a plot at:

» Cemetery Bay, Norfolk Island – (locals only)
» Aslings Beach, Eden, NSW
» Bombo Beach, Kiama, NSW

Indigenous Australians used beaches, particularly
sand dunes, as burial sites.

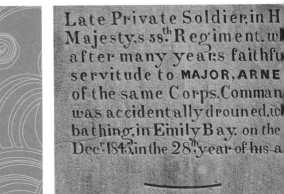

Late Private Soldier, in H
Majesty,s 58th Regiment. w
after many years faithfu
servitude to MAJOR, ARNE
of the same Corps. Comman
was accidentally drouned, w
bathing, in Emily Bay, on the
Decr 1843, in the 28th year of his a

EMILY BAY

CONVICT HISTORY | CALM LAGOON | REMOTE ISLAND LOCATION | HISTORIC CEMETERY

Emily Bay featured very early in the history of Australia's settlement by Europeans. HMS *Supply*, one of the ships of the First Fleet, landed here in March 1788. Its party of 23, including 15 convicts, established the New South Wales colony's second settlement on the then uninhabited island.

Since those first convicts hoed the rich basalt soil to grow food for the starving Sydney Town the island has had a rich history.

From 1825, Norfolk Island was the site of the infamous penal settlement for second offenders, which became a 'hell on earth'. The convicts built the beautiful Georgian military barracks and their own gaol on the shores of Slaughter Bay just to the west of Emily Bay. The well-preserved remnants of the gaol still remain and the original barracks now house government offices.

On the other side of Emily Bay lies Cemetery Bay, where the salt-etched headstones tell many a sad story. As the last of the convicts departed in 1856, the descendants of the *Bounty* mutineers arrived from Pitcairn Island to settle permanently

and establish the idyllic settlement we see today.

Like the rest of the island, Emily Bay itself has an interesting history. Its bordering calcarenite dunes were quarried to build all the major buildings, lime was burnt in a kiln cut into the calcarenite and a salt works was established on the western point. Its concentration pond, cut into the wave-washed rock platform, can still be seen. A windmill stood on the eastern point, where today a lone Norfolk Island pine hangs over the water. Behind the beach lie remnants of an earlier Polynesian settlement as well as the island's golf links.

Emily Bay has a curving 300-metre-long beach sheltered between two low points with a row of the ubiquitous Norfolk Island pines along the low dune at the rear. A continuous beachrock reef 300 metres offshore blocks all waves at low tide, forming a quiet lagoon; a few low waves reach the beach at high tide. Emily Bay is the best of the island's sandy beaches, although surfers head to 'The Reef' nearby and to Anson Bay, in the north-west.

The penal settlement on Norfolk Island was once known as 'hell on earth', but these days the island's beaches are the picture of tranquillity. The best of them is Emily Bay, with its protected lagoon, convict remnants and the historic burial ground at neighbouring Cemetery Bay to explore.

FINGAL BAY NEW SOUTH WALES
HISTORIC LIGHTHOUSE AND RUINS | LOW-TIDE WALK TO ISLAND | SURFING | ROCKS

Fingal Bay forms a perfect semicircle between Point Stephens and Fingal Head in the Hunter region of New South Wales. In the 19th century, the bay was known as False Bay because it was sometimes mistaken for the entrance to Port Stephens. The 1-kilometre-wide entrance opens into a wide bay containing Fingal Beach, which curves round the bay, changing orientation and character along the way.

As you walk northwards along the beach from Fingal Head, the waves gradually increase in size. About halfway along, the road and bike path from Port Stephens end at the beach and this is where you'll find the surf life saving club, parkland, a small commercial centre and a boat ramp. The surf here is usually reasonable and good surf continues around much of the remainder of the beach. Rips are common, so swimmers should stay near the surf club. Along its northern curve, the beach narrows to a sandy isthmus just a few metres wide that separates it from its northern neighbour, Fly Roads. In big seas, this narrow strip of sand is often breached and waves wash between the two beaches. When the isthmus is connected you can continue walking out along 'the spit' at low tide to Point Stephens, which is part of Tomaree National Park, and also to the lighthouse and ruins of the early keeper's residence. But do keep an eye on the tides if you spend a long time on the 'island'. Behind the isthmus is a large area of active bare sand dunes.

At the southern end of the beach, Fingal Head, there is a part-elevated walkway through the native vegetation and, for the more energetic, some rugged rock formations that are worth exploring.

At low tide, you can walk across the sandy isthmus from Fingal Beach to Point Stephens, part of Tomaree National Park. Here, you can wander round the historic lighthouse and ruins of the early keeper's residence. Keep an eye on the water, though, as the point can become an island at high tide.

FOUR MILE BEACH
PORT DOUGLAS, QUEENSLAND

TROPICAL SEAS | COCONUT PALMS | NORTH QUEENSLAND HERITAGE | REEF ADVENTURES

Established as a booming goldfields port in the 1880s and at one time boasting 48 'pubs' (many were just lean-to tents), Port Douglas then declined for a century into a sleepy sugarcane town. But in recent decades it has been transformed into a global tourist destination that owes much of its popularity to the beautiful Four Mile Beach on its eastern edge.

The town's bustling main street runs between the port and the northern end of the beach. At this end you'll find a series of resorts, large and small, and other accommodation. Largely developed since the 1980s when new coastal planning regulations controlled development, the buildings are no higher than the swaying coconut palms and are tucked behind a generous fringe of tropical coastal vegetation – a green curtain that runs the length of the beach.

This set-back style of coastal planning, now used in other developments along the east coast, not only maintains the natural feel of the beach but also provides a protective buffer from cyclones.

This beach itself has fine sand (a mixture of off-white silica, shell and coral grit) and a shallow surf zone, with generally low-spilling waves generated by the trade winds. There is a surf life saving club and stinger enclosure at the northern end.

Early morning sees both locals and visitors strolling the beach and northern headland or enjoying the sunrise from under the palm fronds. Sunbathers and water enthusiasts visit throughout the day but, for many, sunset is the favourite time of day around here.

The township is a rich blend of new and old, including the original pub, a real north Queensland classic, and the old sugar jetty. The dazzling marina is filled with luxurious charter cruisers that can take you out on a reef adventure.

Low-rise development has preserved the natural feel of Port Douglas' Four Mile Beach, where the buildings hide behind swaying coconut palms and the fringe of tropical vegetation backing the beach. The town is a rich blend of new and old, including the original pub, a real north Queensland classic, and the old sugar jetty.

FRANGIPANI BEACH
CAPE YORK, QUEENSLAND

AUSTRALIA'S NORTHERNMOST TIP | EPIC ROAD ADVENTURE | TORRES STRAIT SUNSETS

At the northernmost tip of Australia, beautiful Frangipani Beach is a great place to cool off after the epic two to three-day 4WD trek from Cooktown. The rough dirt road includes more than 30 creek and river crossings, some the habitat of crocodiles.

Frangipani Beach is located at the very northern tip of Australia at the end of a torturous two-to-three day, 750-kilometre trek by 4WD. Completing this trip is the golden chalice of many an off-road driver. The often-rutted dirt road from Cooktown to Cape York includes more than 30 creek and river crossings, some the habitat of crocodiles. The road ends among the trees at the eastern end of the beach and most travellers park here then either cross the beach at low tide or, at high tide, walk along the rocky cape to reach the very tip of Cape York – Australia's northernmost point.

The beautiful cream-coloured beach faces north-west out across Torres Strait with its back to the prevailing south-east trade winds. A fringe of casuarinas overhangs the gently curving beach. As the tide retreats, it reveals a 250-metre-wide stretch of clean sand capped by several sand ridges. Waves are usually low to calm and the trade winds blowing offshore can produce glassy conditions. After the epic journey to the Cape, Frangipani is a great place to camp, swim and enjoy the golden tropical sunsets over Torres Strait.

While at the cape visit the ruins at nearby Somerset, a settlement set up by the pioneering Jardine brothers in the 1860s. It was intended to rival Singapore, a venture that obviously failed. Also worth a visit are the Aboriginal and Islander communities of Bamaga, where you'll find Australia's northernmost mainland pub as well as the delightful coastal settlement at Seisia, with its beachfront camping area.

Be warned, though, a trip to the tip of Cape York is rough and it's tough, so plan well before you go. The best time to travel is winter, as sections of the road are closed during the summer wet season. For those who can't face the road trip, there are alternatives, including luxury charter flights from Cairns.

EXTREMITIES

There is a beach at each of Australia's four compass points:

» Frangipani Beach, Cape York, QLD – furthest north
» Little Wategos Beach, Cape Byron, NSW – furthest east
» Home Cove TAS – furthest south
» Steep Point, WA – furthest west

Three of these beaches are difficult to get to. You need a 4WD to reach Frangipani and Steep Point and a boat for Home Cove. But it's only a short walk from neighbouring beaches to reach Little Wategos.

GIBSONS STEPS

DRAMATIC NATIONAL PARK COAST | ERODED SEA STACKS | CLIFF WALKWAY | WILD SURF

Nature is a capricious architect of coastlines, with surf and wind fashioning rocks and cliffs into sculpted forms. One of the world's most dramatic coastal formations is the series of eroded sea stacks off the southern Victorian coast, which includes the 65-metre-high 'Twelve Apostles' as well as those at Gibsons Steps, just a kilometre to the east.

Set within the Port Campbell National Park, this cliff-hanging walkway leads down to the sand from a small car park just off the Great Ocean Road. The beach is set between the base of the sheer cliffs and the relentless seas of the Southern Ocean, making this one of the best spots in Australia to see, close up, high surf and the impact it can have on the beach and the cliffs behind it.

The steps have an interesting history. The traditional inhabitants, the Kirrae Whurrong, cut the original access to the beach to help them forage for food along the seashore. In the 1870s, local settler Hugh Gibson improved the access by cutting steps straight down through the cliffs' soft limestone. Those wet, slippery and dangerous steps have now been replaced by the present safer and more accessible stairs.

When you get down to the beach, stay well clear of the surf if waves are breaking. This is *not* a swimming beach, even in apparently calm conditions as strong surge and rip currents are common. Do, however, walk along the beach to see the eroding cliffs and the wild surf, and admire the two sea stacks close to shore known locally as 'Gog and Magog'. These have formed in the same way as the neighbouring Twelve Apostles. When high waves attack the soft marls it leads to rapid cliff erosion and only the most resilient pieces are left as freestanding sea stacks, striking examples of the power of the ocean.

The two eroded sea stacks known as 'Gog and Magog' are battered by the ferocious surf off Gibsons Steps in Victoria's Port Campbell National Park. Access to the sands is via a dramatic cliff-hanging walkway, but this wild beach is definitely not a place to swim.

COASTAL WALKS

All of the great coastal walks take in a number of beaches. Among the best are:

» Angourie to Station Creek, Yuraygir National Park, NSW – 65 km
» Light to Light, Ben Boyd National Park, NSW – 38 km
» The Wilderness Coast, Croajingolong National Park, VIC – 110 km
» Great Ocean Walk, Cape Otway National Park, VIC – 104 km
» Great Southwest Walk, Discovery Bay National Park, VIC – 250 km loop
» Cape to Cape Walk, Leeuwin-Naturaliste National Park, WA – 135 km

Coastal walks, be they one day or seven, can be one of life's great adventures, but make sure you prepare before you go.

BEACH-SIDE RAIL

If you fancy a train or tram ride to the beach, head for:

» Goolwa, SA – first train in Australia
» Illawarra line, NSW – Stanwell Park to Coalcliff
» Cronulla, NSW
» Cottesloe, WA
» Glenelg, SA
» St Kilda, VIC

At Bombo, NSW, the train station is literally on the beach.

GLENELG ADELAIDE, SOUTH AUSTRALIA

HISTORIC TRAMLINE | URBAN CAFE CULTURE | JETTY PROMENADE | PARKLANDS

When it comes to a traditional seaside experience in almost Victorian style, few beaches can compete with Glenelg. The combination of a tram from the city, a boardwalk and a long walking jetty is a reminder of the beginnings of popular bathing that began in 19th-century England. Transport by train and tram popularised the beach and made the sea and its pleasures accessible and affordable – as is still the case here at Glenelg.

Glenelg was also where, in 1836, the newly appointed surveyor-general, Captain William Light, landed to select a site for the colony of South Australia. The area has been a focal point on the Adelaide coast ever since. A 380-metre-long jetty was built for shipping in 1857, the tramway followed in 1873, Luna Park opened in 1930, the Glenelg Surf Life Saving Club was founded in 1939 and rapid residential development from the 1950s has created today's bustling seaside suburbs.

Adelaide's city beaches extend for 30 kilometres from Seacliff to North Haven. Glenelg sits at the mouth of the Patawalonga River, a centre of beach, boating and recreation activities. The river mouth was redeveloped in the 1990s with a large marina, accommodation, waterfront restaurants and extensive parkland stretching to the south behind the beach.

The beach faces due west onto Gulf St Vincent and is sheltered from most ocean swell. The low gulf waves that lap the beach slowly move sand northward along the shore, forming two sandbars parallel to the shore, their crests exposed at low tide. The sand also piles up on the south side of the river mouth and has to be pumped to the northern side.

Glenelg is where Adelaide's residents and visitors come to be refreshed by the gulf and its waters. The new jetty, built in 1969, extends 215 metres out into the gulf and is a favourite place to stroll. Glenelg offers swimming, boating, fishing and much more, all at the end of a direct tramline from downtown Adelaide.

Adelaide's favourite beach retains something of its history as a 19th-century seaside destination. A leisurely tram ride from the city, Glenelg offers gentle waves and, for those more interested in strolling than swimming, a wide jetty projecting out into Gulf St Vincent.

GODFREYS BEACH TASMANIA

The historic Tasmanian fishing village of Stanley nestles beneath The Nut, a dramatic basalt plug that is all that remains of a once giant volcano. Neighbouring Godfreys Beach also bears evidence of its volcanic past in the eroded basalt boulders that stand at each end.

The Nut at Stanley is one of Tasmania's most recognisable natural features, a 143-metre-high volcanic plug rising dramatically out of the sea on the shores of Bass Strait. Early navigator Matthew Flinders called it 'Circular Head' when, in 1798, he recorded seeing a *'cliffy, round lump, in form much resembling a Christmas Cake'.*

The massive eroded stump of basalt, spectacular from a distance, is all that remains of a once giant volcano. It is fun to explore its steep sides and flat top, either by chairlift or by a winding foot track. The charming historic town of Stanley nestles neatly at its base.

Two fine beaches flank the base of The Nut. The most attractive is Godfreys Beach, on the northern side of the town, a wide swimming, fishing and walking beach that curves gently for a kilometre or so up onto the north headland where the majestic Highfield House is perched.

This building was the base for the powerful Van Diemen's Land Company, an agricultural and pastoral group that opened up Tasmania's north-west from 1826 and still operates today.

Godfreys Beach faces north-east so the prevailing westerlies blow offshore. The waves are usually low and break across a wide shallow bar that fronts the beach and is exposed at low tide. Basalt boulders, eroded from the adjacent headlands, stand at either end. There is a picnic area at the southern end and Stanley's quaint main street is right behind it.

You can follow the main street down to the harbour where the fishing fleet moors at the historic port, which dates back to 1827. A walk around the colourful harbour may bring you face to face with generations of local fishermen who have many tales of the high seas. Some boats still go out for weeks at a time, continuing the proud maritime tradition of this seafaring region.

GREEN PATCH

WHITE SANDS | NATIONAL PARK | KANGAROOS | BIRD LIFE | SNORKELLING | DOLPHINS

Pristine Jervis Bay is a vast beach-rimmed stretch of water that opens to the Tasman Sea between the prominent Point Perpendicular and Bowen Island. This idyllic part of the coast includes several national parks and has a significant and ongoing Aboriginal presence.

Waves enter the bay though the 3-kilometre-wide entrance and spread out around its 47 kilometres of shoreline, resulting in mostly calm waters. The bay is renowned for its crystal-clear waters, fine sands, abundant seagrass meadows and rich marine life. Much of it is protected in the Booderee and Jervis Bay national parks, Jervis Bay Marine Park and Wreck Bay Aboriginal Land.

The bay's 30 beaches are composed of what some say is the whitest sand in Australia (see Whitehaven Beach). All enjoy usually low-lapping waves and calm swimming conditions, but the best of them is at Green Patch in the southern Booderee National Park. This park has an informative visitor centre at its entrance, staffed largely by local Aboriginal rangers.

The popular Green Patch camping area is in a shady spot behind the beach. You will probably share the space with inquisitive kangaroos, noisy kookaburras, colourful rosellas, squawking lorikeets and shy wombats. The marine life is just as rich. The resident dolphins do their daily round of the beaches, in season you can see whales enjoying the deeper waters of the bay and there is a penguin colony on Bowen Island.

The usually calm conditions, clean sand and seagrass growing only 50 metres offshore make this an ideal place to swim, snorkel, kayak and just enjoy the water.

While you're in the region, it's worth exploring the wide range of ocean and bay beaches, walking trails, ruins of the historic lighthouse at Cape St George and coastal views. Boating enthusiasts will find a boat ramp at nearby Murrays Beach.

Green Patch on the shores of Jervis Bay offers clear emerald waters, white sands, and popular National Park campsites, though you may have to share with kangaroos, wombats and a host of birds.

GREENLY BEACH
EYRE PENINSULA, SOUTH AUSTRALIA

WILDERNESS BEACH | DRAMATIC MOUNTAIN BACKDROP | FISHING | SURFING | SHARKS

Some beaches just beg the budding artist to set up an easel and try to capture the coastal landscape and this is one of them. Just 50 kilometres north-west of the tuna capital, Port Lincoln, and 10 kilometres off the highway, Greenly Beach is backed by the imposing Mount Greenly, providing a dramatic backdrop to this raw natural beach. The road runs out to a car park at the southern end of the beach – the only 'footprint' on an otherwise wonderfully undeveloped part of the coast.

The beach is composed entirely of coarse, orange carbonate sand washed up from the sea floor. Because of the size of the grains, the sand maintains a steep swash zone lined by prominent undulating scallops or beach cusps along its crest and dropping suddenly into deeper water at its base. There is an active dune field between the beach and the mountain behind.

Greenly is located on the eastern shores of the Great Australian Bight, which stretches 1000 kilometres to the Western Australia border, and it faces due west into the prevailing swell. It is the first beach north of Coffin Bay to receive regular swell, although still slightly reduced by the Coffin Bay Peninsula. In winter especially, there are some decent beach breaks but, like most beaches in South Australia and particularly in this southern region, Greenly has a reputation for large 'man-eating' sharks. Shark-cage experiences are on

Greenly Beach on South Australia's sparsely populated Eyre Peninsula offers a pristine natural environment with the imposing Mount Greenly providing a dramatic backdrop. Facing due west into the prevailing swell, Greenly offers good surfing, although the area has a reputation for its sharks.

offer in Port Lincoln for thrill-seeking tourists.

This is a popular spot for Port Lincoln locals to swim and picnic, fish and paint. When the swell is over 1 metre there is usually some surf, and accompanying rips, and this attracts a hardened crew of surfers.

GUNYAH BEACH
EYRE PENINSULA, SOUTH AUSTRALIA

WILD NATIONAL PARK BEACH | BIG SURF | BIG DUNES | AUSTRALIA'S BIGGEST RIPS

Gunyah Beach is the highest energy beach on the long western coast of the Eyre Peninsula. Persistent big swells generated by the Southern Ocean average over 2.5 metres and break across a 500-metre-wide surf zone, in the process creating the largest rip currents anywhere in Australia.

Strong onshore winds have also mobilised the fine beach sand and blown it up to 9 kilometres inland, almost as far as the township of Coffin Bay. According to Aboriginal legend, the dunes originated when a great fire here was smothered by sand.

The 15-kilometre-long beach is located in the magnificent Coffin Bay National Park, on a vast T-shaped sand-draped peninsula that anchors the eastern end of the Great Australian Bight. Explorer Matthew Flinders, who visited here in 1802, left us his troubled impressions of the region in his naming of coastal sites like Cape Catastrophe, Anxious Bay, Coffin Bay, Misery Bay and Memory Bay. The latter was the base from which he searched unsuccessfully for seven missing seamen whose names live on in the seven nearby islands he named in their honour.

Access to Gunyah Beach is via a 20-kilometre-long sealed road from Coffin Bay township. The car park at the beach overlooks the more sheltered western end of the beach, where it's called Almonta Beach. The waves may be a little lower here but strong rip currents still dominate the surf zone. As with any dangerous beach, swimming is at one's own risk.

The beach, which can also be reached via a 4WD track through the dunes, is renowned for great fishing in the many rip channels and troughs. This is a difficult and dangerous beach to drive, so use caution if four-wheel-driving to avoid getting bogged.

RIP CURRENTS

On any day there are approximately 17 000 rip currents operating around our coast, most of them around the higher energy southern half of the continent. Rip current spacing – the distance between rip currents along a beach – varies from an average of:

» 100 m across northern Australia (see Mission Beach)
» 250 m along the south-east coast (see Bondi Beach)
» and up to 500 m across the southern coast (see Gunyah Beach)

Rip currents are responsible for over 90 per cent of all beach rescues in Australia. It's easy to panic when caught in a rip, making your situation even more dangerous. Try to concentrate on staying afloat, even if the current carries you some distance from the beach.

Wild Gunyah Beach on the western coast of the Eyre Peninsula has spectacular surf and Australia's biggest rips. Powerful onshore winds have blown the fine beach sand up to 9 kilometres inland, producing the massive white dunes.

HORSESHOE BAY
MAGNETIC ISLAND, QUEENSLAND

NATIONAL PARK | WALKS | SNORKELLING | SEA KAYAKING | FERRY RIDE FROM TOWNSVILLE

Magnetic Island rises 500 metres out of the sea just 7 kilometres east of the north Queensland city of Townsville. 'Maggie' is Townsville's island suburb, home to 2000 people and an ever-popular tourist destination. A regular ferry service runs between the city and the island, transporting you to another world.

More than half the island is national park and the surrounding waters are a marine park. The island boasts 50 kilometres of coast, with sloping granite rocks framing 24 mostly untouched beaches. The sun shines 320 days a year and the temperature of the clean clear water never drops below 28°C.

Horseshoe is the longest and best of the beaches on beautiful Magnetic Island, a short ferry ride from Townsville. Visitors can explore the island's many walking tracks, take a reef cruise or engage in everything from snorkelling to horse riding.

The longest and best of the beaches is Horseshoe Bay, set in an inviting 2-kilometre-wide, north-facing bay. The curving, horseshoe-shaped beach sits between two craggy granite headlands, with the slopes behind rising to the island's peak at Mount Cook. Although the beach is narrow at high tide, it widens as the tide recedes revealing a shallow, usually calm, sandbar at its base.

Leisure boats anchor in the calm waters at the eastern end and the beach offers a range of activities including snorkelling, sailing, diving, horse riding and sea kayaking. Elsewhere on the island, you can rent a small yacht or join a reef cruise. If you settle for a quiet stroll along the beach you may find you have it all to yourself. There are also many island walking tracks to explore, some leading to secluded beaches. Check with locals to find out about the risk of stingers.

There is a range of accommodation and facilities at Horseshoe Bay and across this beautiful island with three other vibrant communities at Arcadia, which includes Alma and Geoffrey bays along with Nelly Bay and Picnic Bay.

The island's name refers to an unexplained, apparently 'magnetic' effect the large lump of granite had on the ship's compass when navigator and explorer James Cook sailed past while making his way up the east coast in 1770.

JOHANNA BEACH

NATIONAL PARK | WILD WINDS | BIG SURF | BIG RIPS | BEACH FISHING | SHIPWRECK COAST

Probably Victoria's most dangerous beach, spectacular Johanna faces squarely into the raging seas of the Southern Ocean along that state's 'Shipwreck Coast'. Although the beach is popular with surfers and beach fishers, be warned that conditions can be extremely hazardous.

Not so much breezy as wildly windswept, Johanna Beach is probably the highest energy and most dangerous beach in Victoria. However it is this raw energy that attracts people to this straight 3.5-kilometre-long beach that faces squarely into the raging seas and relentless swells of the Southern Ocean.

It was these same wild seas that wrecked the locally built schooner *Johanna* here in 1843, imprinting its name on the beach. Johanna is right in the middle of Victoria's 'Shipwreck Coast', site of more than 50 shipwrecks, which stretches for 130 kilometres from Moonlight Head to Cape Otway. Early navigator Matthew Flinders, who sailed past here in the *Investigator* in 1802, wrote: 'I have seldom seen a more fearful section of coastline.'

You can reach Johanna Beach, located in the Great Otway National Park, via a loop road off the Great Ocean Road and it is a detour well worth taking. The road ends at a beachside car park and informal camping area behind a fringe of dunes. Most of the campers here are fishers, surfers or hikers trekking the Great Ocean Walk.

Surf and rock fishers come here to fish the deep holes for snapper, salmon and mulloway year-round. Surfers are drawn to the consistent surf that breaks over a series of sandbars, each separated by deep rip channels. The surf is known for quick increases in wave size – it is reputedly capable of doubling in the space of a few hours. Because of its reliable surf, Johanna is the backup site for the Bells Beach Easter Festival (see Bells Beach).

The semi-permanent rip channels that dominate this beach help to provide the great surf and fishing, but conditions are extremely hazardous for the unwary, so take great care if swimming. The warning signs say it all: 'High surf, submerged rocks, dangerous currents'.

NATIONAL SURFING RESERVES

Australia currently has 18 National Surfing Reserves:

» Burleigh Heads, Currumbin, Snapper–Kirra, QLD
» Lennox Head, Angourie, Crescent Head, Merewether,
  North Narrabeen, Manly–Freshwater, Maroubra, Cronulla,
  Killalea, NSW
» Phillip Island, VIC
» Daly Head, Point Sinclair, SA
» Margaret River, Yallingup, Kalbarri, WA

In 2012, Manly and Freshwater beaches were also
declared Australia's first World Surfing Reserve.

KALBARRI WESTERN AUSTRALIA

RIVER ESTUARY | CLIFFSCAPE | SWIMMING HOLES | NATIONAL SURFING RESERVE

Kalbarri, a growing coastal town of 3000 people, sits at the winding estuarine mouth of the Murchison River, the second longest river in Western Australia. It has become a popular tourist destination, thanks to its beautiful coastline and hospitable locals.

A section of cliffed coast to the south of the town is included in the Kalbarri National Park and boasts spectacular red sandstone cliffs and rock platforms, best viewed from the cliff-top Bigurda walking trail. North of the cliffs, is the 5-kilometre-long beach, divided by protruding reefs into three sections, all of which are close to the road and car parks. The mostly steep beach is composed of relatively coarse sand and has surging waves that wash up the beach face, although the inshore reefs usually keep the waves low close to shore.

The most famous stretch of the beach in surfing circles is the middle section, known as Jakes or Jacques Point, which is renowned for its powerful left point break and pink-garnet-tinted sands. This is one of the first accessible places north of Perth where the full force of the Indian Ocean swell reaches the coast, producing some excellent surf and it is now part of Kalbarri National Surfing Reserve.

The southern stretch of the beach, known as Nancy Beach, is more sheltered, nestling in the lee of Red Bluff. The northern stretch is known as Blue Holes thanks to a series of gaps in the inshore reef that create sheltered tidal pools and small lagoons that are popular with snorkellers.

Although waves may be low at the shore be careful swimming at Kalbarri because there are strong permanent rip currents among the reefs and, in bigger seas, there can be a heavy shore break.

The beach at Kalbarri sits at the estuarine mouth of the Murchison River and is divided into three parts by protruding reefs. The central section, Jakes, is a favourite of surfers while the northern Blue Holes features a series of tidal pools behind the sheltering reefs that make it popular with snorkellers.

KITTY MILLER BAY
PHILLIP ISLAND, VICTORIA

SHIPWRECK | ROCK FORMATIONS | REEF SNORKELLING | MARINE LIFE | CALM WATERS

Secluded Kitty Miller Bay, an almost circular sheltered cove, is the most picturesque and safest of the 22 beaches that line the exposed southern shores of Phillip Island. The curving beach occupies the northern half of the round bay with a grassy foredune providing a natural backdrop. A 200-metre-wide, reef-choked entrance usually allows only low waves to enter the bay, although they can be a little higher at high tide.

Surfers venture out to Kennon Point to surf the right-hand break over the entrance reef. Be careful if swimming away from shore because a strong rip current does flow out on the eastern side of the bay entrance.

Families come here to picnic and swim in the calm inner waters, or to snorkel out over the reef-filled bay floor. At low tide on the eastern rock platform, you can catch a glimpse of the ghostly shipwreck of the three-masted SS *Speke,* wrecked here in 1906 – a reminder of the many wrecks littering the Victorian coastline. The Kitty Miller Shipwreck Walk (2 kilometres return) starts at the car park at the rear of the beach, just off the main Back Beach Road.

To either side of the bay there are extensive columnar basalt rock platforms, narrow ridges of basalt known as dykes, raised boulder beaches and sea stacks, which are well worth exploring at low tide. The rich marine life that thrives in this rocky bay also finds its way to the beach, providing a

treasure trove of interesting flotsam.

The beach lies next door to Summerland Bay, Victoria's most-visited beach thanks to its famous evening penguin parade. Just on dusk every evening, thousands of the small 'Little' or 'Fairy' penguins – they grow to a mere 33 centimetres in height – waddle up the beach to their burrows in the sand dunes at the back of Summerland Beach, watched by thousands of sightseers.

This charming beach on Phillip Island's
southern shore owes its calm waters
to the encircling headlands and rocky
reef-filled entrance. For snorkellers,
the reef offers plentiful marine life
while walkers may prefer to follow
the short trail leading to a ghostly
view of the SS *Speke*, wrecked here
in 1906.

LIPSON COVE EYRE PENINSULA, SOUTH AUSTRALIA

WHITE SANDS | BUSH CAMPING | WILDLIFE | DOLPHINS | LOW-TIDE WALK TO ISLAND

South Australia's Eyre Peninsula offers a majestic 770-kilometre coastal drive along the Lincoln and Flinders highways, fringed by hundreds of mostly empty beaches. One of the best on the eastern side of the peninsula is the coastal hideout of Lipson Cove, located 7 kilometres off the highway about an hour north of Port Lincoln. The cove was once the port for a nearby talc mine and there was a small settlement here. The jetty was demolished in 1949.

The cove is sheltered by the small Lipson Island, a conservation park, which is almost connected to the mainland. In fact, you can wade across to the island at low tide. In the other direction, the beach curves to the north for just over 1 kilometre to a small northern headland. Low, partly vegetated dunes back the beach, which is composed of pure white silica

sand derived from the granite hills behind. The fine sand produces a firm compact beach, suitable for driving and parking, like a number of South Australian hard-packed sand beaches (see Long Beach). A basic camping area lies behind the dunes at the southern end of the beach.

Lipson Island is home to a rich ecosystem including 20 endangered bird, mammal and plant species. Marine life is also abundant and eleven species of whale and dolphin have been recorded near the island. Dolphins in particular are a common sight in the cove.

Lipson is a great place to camp, picnic, swim, fish or explore. When a good swell is running up the gulf there can be low surf here too, so it's worth checking if you are looking for a wave along this usually calm part of the coast.

Deserted Lipson Cove on
South Australia's Eyre
Peninsula is a haven
for wildlife, hosting 20
endangered bird, mammal
and plant species. At low
tide, you can walk to the
offshore Lipson Island, a
conservation park.

LITTLE BEACH
TWO PEOPLES BAY, WESTERN AUSTRALIA

NATURE RESERVE | DUNES | COASTAL CLIFFS AND LAKES | SEASIDE WALKS

This beach may be little, but it makes a big impression. Untouched and dramatic, it encapsulates everything that is special about this stretch of coast in southern Western Australia.

Just 30 minutes from Albany, Little Beach is part of the Two Peoples Bay Nature Reserve, which includes 4700 hectares of rugged Proterozoic granite coastal cliffs and slopes, as well as Holocene and Pleistocene dune systems cradling lakes Gardner and Moates. The road ends at the southern end of Two Peoples Bay beach where there is a visitor centre, picnic ground and boat-launching area. Some 4WD tracks also lead through the reserve to the cliffs above Sinkers Reef and Nanarup Beach and vehicles are permitted along the northern half of Two Peoples Bay beach.

But it is worth driving a kilometre or so east of the visitor centre to find superb Little Beach. This 300-metre curving beach of pure white sand is bounded by sloping headlands and backed by towering granite ridges. Two large boulders pin-point the centre of the beach. Waves are usually low, the water crystal clear and the beach faces north-east into the sun.

Wander round the eastern rocks and you will find a smaller replica, an 80-metre-long pocket of similar white sand, with its centre boulder lying 50 metres offshore. Head west and you can follow the Heritage Trail past a tidal pool to a sheltered rock-enclosed beach that is actually a sand flat surrounded by freshwater reeds. This trail wanders all the way back to the visitor centre.

This is a place to clamber over the boulders, swim, snorkel and just enjoy the pristine natural beauty of this superb part of the coast.

With its clear waters and stunning coastal scenery, Little Beach in southern Western Australia makes a big impression. The beach is part of the Two Peoples Bay Nature Reserve, which features rugged granite coastal cliffs and dunes that shelter two coastal lakes.

LONG BEACH ROBE, SOUTH AUSTRALIA

HISTORIC FISHING PORT | LOCAL CRAYFISH | WHITE SANDS | BEACH DRIVING | SURFING

Six thousand years ago, as the sea level rose, it partly drowned an ancient dune system, now known as the Robe Range, breaching the dunes at the northern end to form the 10-kilometre-wide Guichen Bay.

The shelter provided by the bay led in 1847 to the establishment of the port of Robe, once one of the busiest in Australia. Many of this charming village's stone buildings and houses date from the 1840s. The port originally shipped wool but today is a centre for professional fishing and crayfishing – so watch out for catches of the famous local southern rock lobster.

Sheltered within the bay, the shoreline gradually built out 4 kilometres into the sea to form today's curving Long Beach. The beach's fine, firm white sand is made up of broken-down carbonate detritus, the remains of marine organisms that form many of the beaches and dunes across southern Australia. The rock reefs fringing the bay keep waves low along the shore, producing wide, gentle surf.

The beach is firm enough for regular vehicle traffic and is an official 'road' with a 20 km/h speed limit and parking. In summer, it is often lined with rows of cars as beachgoers place their towels and picnic gear next to their vehicles and stroll to the surf. This is the easiest and best beach driving in South Australia.

South of the town, the Robe Range extends along the coast creating a rugged rocky shoreline that contains scores of small beaches. Some are accessible by car, including the interesting shack community at Nora Creina, an almost circular sheltered bay. Robe is ideal for a weekend escape from Adelaide and is a great base to explore the this fascinating region.

Long Beach, near the historic fishing port of Robe, is designated an official road, thanks to its firm white sands. This is the easiest and best beach driving in South Australia.

LORNE GREAT OCEAN ROAD, VICTORIA

SCENIC BEACH | FISHING PORT | CAFE LIFESTYLE | FOREST BACKDROP | COASTAL DRIVE

Victoria's Great Ocean Road is one of the world's best coastal drives and the beautiful holiday village of Lorne is a highlight along the way. Visitors can ride the usually gentle surf, enjoy the many cafes and restaurants, or explore the towering temperate rainforests of the neighbouring Otway Ranges.

Two and a half hours from Melbourne, Lorne is one of Victoria's favourite summer destinations, accessed via the spectacular Great Ocean Road. Soldiers returned from WWI built the road between 1919 and 1932, opening up this once inaccessible stretch of coast and creating one of the great ocean drives in the world. Part of the National Heritage List, the Great Ocean Road is also the world's largest monument to those who served in WWI. This dramatic piece of engineering winds along precipitous coastal cliffs, around headlands, beside beaches, across rivers and estuaries and through mountains that are home to Australia's tallest rainforests.

With the improved access, the first guesthouses opened in Lorne in the 1930s and the surf life saving club followed in 1948. The town's continuing popularity is due to a combination of its beautiful beach, long sheltering headland, wide foreshore reserve and the forested slopes rising into the Otway Ranges behind. The foreshore contains parking, the surf club, extensive grassy picnic areas and a resort. The reserve extends out along the point where there is a shady walking track and more parking and picnic areas.

The beach is sheltered by Point Grey, once the town's port and still home to its fishing fleet and jetty. The persistent swell from the Southern Ocean wraps round the point and, lowered in height, arrives in straight lines at the wide firm beach to break gently across the broad shallow sandbar. The beach extends north to the mouth of the Erskine River, which is usually blocked, and is patrolled in summer by lifeguards and the surf club.

LUCKY BAY WESTERN AUSTRALIA

WHITE SANDS | NATIONAL PARK WILDERNESS | SNORKELLING | WILDFLOWERS | WALKS

Lucky Bay is where the explorer John Eyre, got 'lucky' in 1841 when, after four months of trekking along the edge of the Great Australian Bight and the loss of three companions, he came upon the whaling ship *Mississippi* at anchor – a meeting that probably saved his life. Today, this region is still in a mostly natural state, protected within the Cape Le Grande National Park. The park extends along 78 kilometres of coast and has 27 beaches, the pick of which is Lucky Bay, although there could be many deserving runners up here.

As the road gently descends into this deep aqua bay, it offers a view along the 3.5-kilometre-long, white-sand beach. It's a refreshing sight for those who've driven across the Nullarbor or who have made the long drive down from Perth via Esperance.

The bay finishes at either end with rounded granite boulders and headlands. Granite dominates this section of coast and supplies the silica that creates the dazzling sands. Lucky Bay is one of the beaches to claim the title of whitest sand in Australia (see Whitehaven Beach).

The sheltered western end of the bay has usually low to calm waves with seagrass growing to the shore. This is where the camping and picnic areas are located and is one of the best places to swim, snorkel, picnic and meet the local kangaroos. As you move east along the beach, the waves begin to pick up and, within 500 metres of the eastern headland, rip currents become common. This is where the fishers and surfers head, finding reasonable surf and plenty of gutters all the way to the end of the beach.

There is much to do in this area, including bushwalking and climbing the several tall peaks in the park. Wildflowers carpet the coastline during spring and those photogenic kangaroos hang out on the beach all year round.

Pristine Lucky Bay, in the Cape Le Grande National Park, is a refreshing sight for those who've just driven across the Nullarbor to Western Australia. This is one of several beaches to claim the title of whitest sand in the country.

MANDALAY BEACH WESTERN AUSTRALIA

SHIPWRECK I DUNES I WILD SEAS I BIG RIPS I STUNNING SCENERY

This beach is not on every traveller's checklist. Along this stretch of coast, there are a number of vaguely marked turn-offs that could lead you on a longish return trip to nowhere of real interest but the 7-kilometre road to Mandalay, off the South-Western Highway near Walpole, is one detour that will not disappoint. This is simply a superb, natural ocean beach.

A Norwegian ship driven ashore and wrecked here in 1911 lent its name to this dramatic beach, and parts of the wreck are still occasionally exposed by moving sand. Mandalay is typical of many of the high-energy beaches that line Western Australia's southern coast. An elevated walking platform at the western end provides a view right along the beach and seaward to the conical wave-washed

Dramatic Mandalay Beach owes its name to a Norwegian ship wrecked here in 1911, parts of which are still occasionally exposed by the shifting sands. Visitors can view the wild seas and large beach rips from the elevated walking platform at the western end, but should be aware that swimming here can be dangerous.

Chatham Island. If you continue along the platform you can take the steps down to the golden sand.

The beach faces squarely into the prevailing south-west swell and winds. The swell maintains a series of 4 to 5 large beach rips that flow seaward through the wide surf zone. These rip channels are great for beach fishing and can at times provide good surf, but swimming is not recommended. The channels are easily visible from the platform and should be noted and avoided. When a strong wind is blowing it sends sand from the beach onto the high grassy foredune and, in the centre, into elongated sand blowouts.

All in all, isolated Mandalay Beach is the best of the pristine, exposed surf beaches with active dunes along this section of coast.

MOST HAZARDOUS (RATING 1-10)

The big waves of southern Australia result in many hazardous beaches with 101 beaches rated 10 or extremely hazardous. Of the beaches in this book, the most hazardous are:

» Ocean Beach, TAS – (10)
» Mandalay, WA – (9)
» Gunyah, SA – (8)
» Portsea, VIC – (8)

Portsea is the most hazardous patrolled beach in Australia.

MANLY BEACH SYDNEY, NEW SOUTH WALES

URBAN CAFE LIFE | SEASIDE PROMENADE | SURFING HERITAGE | WORLD SURFING RESERVE

Manly on Sydney's North Shore is where Australian surfing really started and it is still the favourite surfing beach of Sydneysiders. A ferry ride from the centre of town, the beach became Australia's first World Surfing Reserve in 2012.

Lively Manly Beach offers a more or less continuous beach parade, especially at the height of summer. Along with Bondi, Noosa and Surfers Paradise, it is one of the four favourite beach destinations on the east coast.

For over 160 years, Manly has been one of the most popular beaches in Australia. It's here that 'surf bathing' really started and the essential threads of surfing history were sewn into the nation's beach-culture fabric.

It was also one of the first places in Australia to be named by resident Europeans. In 1788, while searching for fresh water for the fledgling colony at Sydney Cove, Governor Arthur Phillip observed of the local Aboriginal people: 'their confidence and manly behaviour made me give the name of Manly Cove to this place.'

Englishman Henry Gilbert Smith established a guesthouse here in the 1880s and started publicising Manly as a seaside resort – an escape by ferry from dusty Sydney Town. Not much has changed. The ever-popular Manly ferry

transports thousands of people each day between the city and the sea and the walk along the Corso from the ferry to the beach is a quintessential Sydney experience. Despite considerable development, Manly retains its vibrant beach and surf environment and is clearly the favourite surfing beach of Sydneysiders. The beach is clean, open and consistently wave-lashed – you will see surfers here from dawn to dusk.

A broad shady esplanade with a continuous seawall, wide grassy reserve and more than 250 majestic Norfolk Island pines provides a backdrop to the curving shoreline and runs the length of the beach, linking Queenscliff, North Steyne and Manly. Locals jog, cycle and weave their way through the sunburnt throngs.

In recognition of its long and rich surfing tradition, Manly was proclaimed a National Surfing Reserve in 2010 and Australia's first World Surfing Reserve in 2012. It also claims many other 'firsts': beach resort, body-surfing, board surfing, surf club, surf boat, surf carnival and first world surf championships (1964).

MARRAWAH BEACH TASMANIA

REMOTE BEACH | SURFING | HIGH WINDS | FOSSILS | ABORIGINAL CARVINGS

This remote beach is named after the nearby small town, the westernmost in Tasmania and the furthest from both Hobart and Launceston. It's little wonder the beach is often deserted. But thanks to the winds that sweep across 15 000 kilometres of uninterrupted ocean, Marrawah offers the best surf on the island state's west coast, attracting cold-water surfers from across Tasmania.

The beach is sheltered by Green Point, from where it curves for 6 kilometres to the north. The road from town winds down to the southern end of the beach where there's a car park, small camping area and amenities block. The best surf is usually to be found towards this end of the beach. When it's too windy, wind and kite surfing take over. Waves and rip currents dominate most of the beach but the southern rock reefs enclose a 50-metre-long pocket of sand that offers a quieter spot for swimming. The rock is a cemented former beach, known as 'beachrock' and if you look closely you will see many fossilised shells.

At its northern end, the beach ends at the base of Mount Cameron West (170 metres), a massive peak of basalt where there are important Aboriginal carvings. A few vegetated sand dunes extend in from the beach, interlaced with cleared grazing land. Those who like an invigorating walk along the beach could head south to neighbouring Periwinkle Beach.

There are a few remote crayfishing settlements clustered to the south of Marrawah, beyond Arthur River down to Temma. These windswept, craggy outposts are exposed to the wind and waves of the wild west coast and the hardy sea families there claim to have the 'cleanest air on earth'.

This remote beach in western Tasmania is often deserted, but the strong winds and natural environment make it a great place for invigorating walks. The southern beachrock reefs enclose a calmer pocket of water for those who don't want to venture into the surf.

MEELUP WESTERN AUSTRALIA

CALM WATERS | SHADY PICNIC AREA | BOAT ANCHORAGE | MOONRISE OVER GEOGRAPHE BAY

Cape Naturaliste, named by French explorer Nicolas Baudin in 1801, is one of the more prominent landmarks on the Australian coast. From here to that other great landmark, Cape Leeuwin in the Margaret River region far to the south, the 'cape-to-cape' coast offers some of the best surf in the world – not to mention the wines (see Smiths Beach).

Meelup Beach is a local favourite and for good reason. It's safe, protected, shady and close to many other attractions, including delightful Dunsborough. Access is easy, with the Meelup road running right to the beach. Huge waves pound the western side of the cape, but the sheltered eastern side is usually calm with low waves gently lapping against the quiet shores or breaking across a shallow sandbar.

Set in the Meelup Regional Park and located between sloping granite points, the

beach faces north-east into broad Geographe Bay with the prevailing south-westerlies blowing offshore. The shelter afforded by the beach's orientation and backing slopes allows trees to grow right down to the shore, providing a shady canopy over a large grassy picnic area that backs the beach. Its east-facing orientation also gave rise to its name, which means 'place of the rising moon'. The local Wardandi people used to sit and watch the moon rise over the waters of Geographe Bay, still an experience to be savoured today.

The sand here is almost pure carbonate derived from the shells of the bay floor. Boats drop anchor off the beach, within an easy swim to shore. The beach is patrolled by lifeguards in summer and is perfect for families, picnickers or anyone who just wants to relax and enjoy its calm waters. The lighthouse up on the cape is also a favourite side trip for visitors.

The sheltered waters of Meelup Beach are protected from the region's pounding surf by Cape Naturaliste. The name means 'place of the rising moon' in the local Wardandi language and visitors can still enjoy the moonrise over Geographe Bay.

MERDAYERRAH SANDPATCH

NULLARBOR, SOUTH AUSTRALIA

NULLARBOR WILDERNESS BEACH | ACTIVE CLIFF-TOP DUNES | LONG VIEWS | STATE BORDER

The great Nullarbor Cliffs extend for 210 kilometres west from Head of Bight to Wilsons Bluff, which marks the border of South Australia and Western Australia. They range from 70 to 90 metres in height with a sheer drop to the wild seas below. The Eyre Highway runs parallel to the cliffs for their entire length and the occasional viewing spots are highlights along the seemingly endless, relatively featureless drive across the scrubby Nullarbor Plain.

The unsignposted Merdayerrah Sandpatch is the westernmost beach in South Australia. It is known by its Aboriginal name 'Merdayerrah', while 'sandpatch' refers to the climbing dunes that back most of the beach.

It's one of Australia's most fascinating coastal features – and here's why. The sandpatch starts at a sudden offset in the cliffs 27 kilometres east of the border. It heads west in a relatively straight line of calcarenite slopes and bluffs, with increasing patches of sandy beach all the way to the border. The sandpatch and backing slopes represent successive beaches and dunes deposited over the past few hundred thousand years each time the sea level rose to its present level. During each event the wind built sand ramps, which in places reached the top of the 90-metre-high cliffs and blew some distance inland, forming cliff-top dunes. This is one of only a handful of cliff-top dunes that are still active on the Australian coast.

To see the sandpatch, head to one of the small parking areas just off a bend in the highway at 13 kilometres and at 16 and 25 kilometres east of Border Village, each of which provides views from the bluffs down along the beach. Behind the village, a track winds through the scrub for 5 kilometres out to Wilsons Bluff where a rock cairn marks the border of South Australia and Western Australia and the western end of the sandpatch. The bluff here provides both a view east along Merdayerrah, as well as west into Western Australia and the even more massive Eucla sand dunes.

The westernmost beach in South Australia, remote Merdayerrah is one of the few beaches that breaks the monotony of the Nullarbor Plain, most of which is lined with cliffs. It is also known for its active cliff-top dunes and long views towards the even more massive sand dunes of Eucla in Western Australia.

MERIMBULA–PAMBULA
NEW SOUTH WALES

PRISTINE BEACH | FORESTED DUNES | SURFING | HISTORIC JETTY | LOCAL OYSTERS | WALKS

The holiday town of Merimbula is famous for its oysters, surfing and nearby national parks. Its ocean beach is shared with the quieter town of Pambula to the south.

Merimbula–Pambula beach is a gently curving, east-facing stretch of sand that links the two contrasting South Coast communities of Merimbula and Pambula. At both ends, the 6-kilometre beach ends with a river mouth and prominent headland. It is largely in a pristine natural state, and so are its backing low dunes, which are covered in a littoral eucalyptus forest.

At the Merimbula end, the popular, thriving township swells during summer as thousands arrive to holiday here. There is a wide range of accommodation, restaurants and amenities and the town is famous for its local oysters. The equally famous Merimbula sandbar provides consistent long waves, which is why this is the site of the long-running Merimbula Classic surf contest held each November. The beach picks up the southerly swell, which combines with the fine sand to produce a 150-metre-wide double bar surf zone. Rip currents are common along the length of the beach so swim only at the ends of the beach and when they are patrolled.

You can walk out along the rich red shale of the headland and also visit the historic Merimbula jetty and store, which is now a gallery. Merimbula Lake, behind the beach, is a haven for birds and for the kangaroos and wallabies that graze on its shores. It's also the site of the oyster farms.

At the southern end you'll find the more laid-back historic community of Pambula located inland from its beach. At the beach itself there is a surf life saving club, which dates back to 1930, and a beachfront caravan park. Pambula, too, has a famous surf break over the river-mouth shoals. On the southern side of the river mouth is Haycock Point, the northern boundary of Ben Boyd National Park, from which you can enjoy superb views of the entire beach.

Darwin's vibrant Mindil Beach is home to one of Australia's best markets, featuring tropical produce, lively beats and some colourful Top End personalities. Visitors can sit on the sand to eat while watching the sun set over the Timor Sea.

MINDIL BEACH DARWIN, NORTHERN TERRITORY

TWILIGHT MARKETS | TROPICAL PRODUCE | MUSIC | PEOPLE WATCHING | TIMOR SEA SUNSETS

Exotic food, buzzing crowds and tropical sunsets: Darwin's Mindil Beach has a vibe like no other in Australia. It's a multicultural feast of freewheeling characters under a canopy of coconut palms. On Thursday and Sunday nights from May to October, Mindil offers perhaps Australia's, and definitely the Territory's, best market. It's a heady mix of the Top End, the tropics and the orient, with the produce, beats and colourful people to match.

The kilometre-long beach is set between two low headlands, and is steep at high tide. As the tide recedes, it reveals a wider beach. Swimming is best at mid to high tide. Watch for stingers and if you believe the locals (after all, the surf club has one in its emblem), the occasional curious crocodile. Conditions are usually calm with the trade winds blowing offshore and the beach is patrolled by the Mindil Beach Surf Life Saving Club.

The market extends along the rear of the beach and many people wander down and sit on the sand to watch the sun set over the Timor Sea while they eat. During the day, every day, Mindil is Darwin's most accessible and most popular beach at just over 1 kilometre from the city centre.

MISSION BEACH QUEENSLAND

SWAYING PALMS | ISLAND VIEWS | REEF WALKING | KAYAKING | DIVING | NIGHTLIFE

Mission Beach, midway between Townsville and Cairns, used to be right off the beaten track. The site of an Aboriginal mission in the early 1900s, the area was home to little more than small-scale agricultural activities until the 1970s when better access led to the first tourist development.

The beach runs between Clump and Tam O'Shanter points and is backed by coconut palms and a vegetated foredune. There are views of

Dunk Island, just 4 kilometres offshore. The island provides some shelter and low waves usually lap against a steep beach at high tide and break over a wide flat one at low tide.

The beach has three communities, each separated from its neighbour by a tidal creek. North Mission Beach is the centre of the nightlife, with restaurants, bars and a range of accommodation. Central Wongaling Beach is more residential and is home to the surf life

saving club and some tourist facilities. South Mission Beach has a beachfront caravan park, hilltop resort and the Kennedy Walking Track, which leads south to Lovers Beach, Lugger Bay and Tam O'Shanter Point. Waves are also slightly higher here if you are looking for a little surf. Other walking tracks in the mountains behind give great views out to Dunk and Family islands. North of Clump Point, there is a delightful coastal walk to the pocket Bingal Bay and Garners Beach.

A shallow reef runs from Clump Point down to the mouth of Porters Creek and it is well worth exploring when the tide is very low. For the more active Mission Beach also offers sea kayaking, jet skiing, scuba diving, snorkelling, sailing, fishing and croc spotting. And for the *very* active there is skydiving and white-water rafting.

Midway between Townsville and Cairns, tropical Mission Beach offers everything from a natural reef experience to lively restaurants and bars. Coastal and mountain walks give spectacular views of the coast and off-shore islands.

MON REPOS QUEENSLAND

TURTLE NESTING SITE | ROCK POOLS | MANGROVES | LAGOON | KANAKA HERITAGE

The site of the largest loggerhead turtle nesting site in Australia, on most nights in summer Mon Repos sees about 450 turtles come ashore to lay their eggs in holes they dig on the sandy beach. Protected within the Mon Repos Conservation Park, the once endangered turtles are experiencing a slow comeback.

Its name means 'my rest' in French, but Mon Repos could easily be called Turtle Beach. This is the site of the largest loggerhead turtle nesting site in Australia. Protected within the Mon Repos Conservation Park, the once endangered turtle populations are experiencing a slow comeback.

Under cover of darkness, an ancient ritual unfolds on most nights between November and March. Up to 450 loggerhead, flatback and green turtles can be seen coming ashore to lay their eggs in holes they excavate in the sandy beach. About eight weeks later, the hatchlings emerge and make their dash to the open sea.

Mon Repos is the longest beach on the 25-kilometre Bundaberg Coast. Facing north-east, it extends for 1.8 kilometres between low basalt headlands with boulder fields to either side. The sandy beach is relatively steep at high tide, but low tide reveals a usually continuous, attached sand bar. This is a place for beach walks, fossicking in tidal rock pools and swimming in the warm Coral Sea. Waves are usually low but there may be surf during occasional periods of higher swell.

A 150-metre-wide vegetated foredune, where the turtles nest, backs the entire beach and behind that sugarcane grows on the rich basaltic soils. The park also protects remnants of the once extensive Woongarra scrub, mangroves and a tidal lagoon.

A basalt wall here was built in the late 19th century by Kanaka labourers who were recruited mainly from the Solomon and Loyalty islands to work in Queensland's sugarcane fields.

During the nesting season, access is controlled by the park and all visitors to the beach between 6 pm and 6 am must be part of a guided tour. At all other times, there is open access to the park and information centre.

BEST WILDLIFE

Wildlife has adapted to, or ignored, the human presence on many Australian beaches. These are some of the best places to meet the locals (and please observe all signage about interaction with native wildlife):

» Cape Hillsborough, QLD – kangaroos
» Etty Bay, QLD – cassowaries
» Lucky Bay, WA – kangaroos
» Mon Repos, QLD – turtles
» Pebbly Beach, NSW – kangaroos
» Seal Bay, Kangaroo Island, SA – seals

Crocodiles are found on most northern Australia beaches in summer!

MYALL BEACH DAINTREE, QUEENSLAND

Myall Beach on the southern side of Cape Tribulation is where two World Heritage Areas meet: the Daintree Rainforest and the Great Barrier Reef. The Daintree is one of the world's most ancient ecosystems while the beach's coral reefs are part of the richest and most diverse reef system in the world.

Myall Beach is where one of the world's oldest living ecosytems, the Daintree Rainforest, meets the fringing corals of the Great Barrier Reef. This is the place where two World Heritage Areas meet – a rare combination indeed.

The beach lies on the southern side of Cape Tribulation, named by navigator James Cook in 1770 because beyond here all his 'tribulations' began, starting with the holing of his ship on Endeavour Reef.

Today the cape is a magnet for those wanting to experience tropical north Queensland at its best and Myall Beach is the ideal place to do that. It has clean cream sand and crystal-clear waters during the winter season. Its fringing coral reefs are separated by deeper channels where you can drop a line or, if you prefer, kayak or snorkel above the teeming marine life. This is part of the richest and most diverse coral-reef system in the world

and one of the few places where you can drive your car to within metres of the reef. The best access is at the Dubuji picnic area, from which you can take the shortcut straight to the sand or meander along the 1200-metre-long boardwalk through the rich tropical wetland drained by one of the two creeks that cross the beach.

The ancient tropical rainforest on the slopes behind is home to more than 80 of the world's 125 rarest species of plants.

The surrounding area offers a range of quality accommodation, most of it hidden in the rainforest. Scuba diving, four-wheel drive trips, horse riding, rainforest walks, 'jungle surfing' in the rainforest canopy and crocodile cruises are just some of the activities on offer. But, remember, this location is in the wet tropics so check the season and pack some wet-weather gear just in case. Also, observe the crocodile and stinger warning signs.

NEDS BEACH

LORD HOWE ISLAND, NEW SOUTH WALES

WORLD HERITAGE ISLAND | TOWERING MOUNTAINS | PALM FORESTS | CORAL REEF | WALKS

With its towering basalt mountains and forests of kentia palms, the Pacific Ocean paradise of Lord Howe Island offers a real escape from the modern world. The best of its 15 beaches is Neds on the island's north-east corner, with a fringing coral reef that offers great conditions for swimming and snorkelling.

The island paradise of Lord Howe Island, 750 kilometres north-east of Sydney, is dominated by towering basalt mountains and fringed by sandy beaches. Its waters hold the highest-latitude coral-reef system in the world, part of the reason for its World Heritage status. The main reef links the two end points of the island, forming a large lagoon

The island was discovered by Europeans in 1788 when HMS *Supply*, one of the First Fleet ships en route to establish a settlement at Norfolk Island (see Emily Bay) sailed by. But it was not permanently settled until 1834. Today, it has a local population of about 370 and visitor numbers are strictly limited to 400 at any one time.

Lord Howe's shoreline is made up of steep rocky cliffs interspersed with fifteen beaches, of which Neds is the best. Located on the north-east corner of the island, and facing out in that direction, it occupies a semi-circular bay with

steeply vegetated basalt slopes rising at either end.

The curving beach has a fringing coral reef that almost nudges the shoreline, making it perfect for snorkelling and swimming. A shady, well-grassed picnic area includes barbecues, with a kentia palm and banyan fig forest rising behind.

The sand is made up of coral and shell fragments, derived from the reef and ground to a soft golden texture. An intertidal reef platform extends off the eastern headland, further sheltering the cove but also providing a surf break during bigger seas. Waves are usually low to calm at the shore.

There are few vehicles on Lord Howe Island and most people ride bikes or walk. Walking tracks ring the island and also reach the top of Mount Gower (875 metres), a walk that provides stunning views of the island and lagoon. Others take you through the kentia palm forests for which the island is famous and to the remote Boat Harbour boulder beach.

HIDDEN TREASURE

If you are a beachcomber who is looking for more than just driftwood you should visit:

» Armstrong Bay, Warrnambool, VIC – a fabled 16th century Portuguese ship made of mahogany lies hidden in the dunes, last seen in the 1880s

» Guilderton, WA – named after the *Gilt Dragon* wrecked on the beach in 1656 carrying eight chests of gold, which are yet to be found

» Lord Howe Island – a Captain Rattenbury supposedly buried a chest of coins in 1830, which no one has ever found

The biggest treasure find in Australia was the 248 000 silver coins carried by the *Zuytdorp* which was wrecked on the WA coast just south of Shark Bay. Many were recovered and can be seen in the Western Australian Maritime Museum in Fremantle.

Close to the Sydney CBD, the harbour-side beach at Nielsen Park would probably not attract the enthusiastic crowds it does if it were better known by its real name – Shark Beach. However, don't let the name put you off spreading a picnic rug or beach towel and joining the many people who choose its calmer waters and shady parkland over the nearby Bondi Beach (see Bondi Beach).

Generously shaded by grand Moreton Bay figs, Nielsen Park, part of the Sydney Harbour National Park, backs the small 200-metre-long beach, extending inland to the neo-Gothic Victorian sandstone Greycliffe House, built during the 1840s.

Today, beach lovers come, as they have for 100 years, to enjoy the lush green sloping lawns and open areas, the million dollar views across

BEST PICNIC BEACH

If you are looking for a nice shady picnic area right next to the beach, head for:

» The Strand, Townsville, QLD
» Nielsen Park, Sydney Harbour, NSW
» Bridport, TAS
» Meelup Beach, WA
» Mindil Beach, NT

The beach picnic is a quintessential Australian activity. Many popular beaches have shady trees and picnic areas with barbecue facilities.

The sheltered beach at Nielsen Park on the southern shores of Sydney Harbour sees a parade of passing ferries, ships and pleasure craft. A favourite picnic spot for Sydneysiders, Nielsen Park is one of more than 50 pocket beaches spread along both shores of what many consider to be the world's greatest natural harbour.

Sydney Harbour and to cool off in the calm water. On Boxing Day, thousands flock here to watch the start of the Sydney to Hobart yacht race.

The beach (which is protected by a shark net) faces due north across the Harbour, with small sandstone headlands at either end. Sloping into deeper water encircled by the net, it is usually calm, with only the occasional boat's wake disturbing the surface. A stepped seawall backs the beach, along with a café, kiosk, function rooms (many a wedding held here) and changing rooms. For those arriving by boat, there is a drop-off area at the eastern end.

Shark Beach is one of the more than 50 pocket beaches spread along both shores of what many consider to be the world greatest natural harbour.

NINETY MILE BEACH
GIPPSLAND, VICTORIA

WILD SEAS | LONG BEACH | BUSH CAMPING | BIRDS | SEALS | EMUS | ECHIDNAS | LAKES

This majestic, unspoilt beach faces south into Bass Strait, receiving the full force of the gales that thunder in from the west. Australia's third longest uninterrupted beach (see Eighty Mile Beach), it stretches out of sight for 125 kilometres between the northern training walls at Lakes Entrance and the more dynamic McLaughlin Inlet in the south.

The seemingly endless strip of sand formed 6000 years ago when rising sea levels deposited their sediment here, in the process enclosing the Gippsland Lakes, Australia's largest coastal lake system. Constant waves have formed an outer sandbar along the beach, enclosing a deep trough that is usually alive with good eating fish (and sharks).

Ninety Mile is a great wildlife beach, with abundant bird and marine life, kangaroos, emus and echidnas. Seals can often be seen sunning themselves on the sands.

A party of sailors in a longboat was wrecked here in 1797 after escaping a shipwreck on Tasmania's Preservation Island. Stranded without a boat, they had no option but to walk

the 600 kilometres to the infant settlement of Sydney, in what became the first great overland trek by Europeans in Australia. Only three of the 17 sailors survived the epic two-month walk.

Today, Ninety Mile boasts 22 different names along its length, each representing a local area or one of the four small communities that back the beach.

The best way to see it is via the coastal drive that joins the beach 60 kilometres south of Lakes Entrance at Golden Beach, then runs parallel to the shore for 30 kilometres down to the small town of Seaspray. Stop on the drive to climb the foredune for sweeping views along the beach.

Many visitors camp at one of the more than 20 official wilderness-style sites in the scrub behind the protective dune or in the caravan park at Seaspray. If you have a boat, you can also explore the Gippsland Lakes including the 15-kilometre-long Bunga Arm, a narrow channel that backs the northern section of the beach and offers a great sheltered anchorage.

Australia's third longest uninterrupted beach, majestic Ninety Mile faces south into Bass Strait, receiving the full force of the gales that thunder in from the west. Visitors with a boat can explore the calmer Gippsland Lakes that shelter behind the beach's backing dunes.

NORRIES HEAD NEW SOUTH WALES

GENTLE SURF | SHADY CASUARINAS | ROCK PLATFORMS | HEADLAND VIEWS | WHALES

The Tweed Coast in northern New South Wales includes quiet estuaries, small villages and clean wave-washed beaches over about 40 kilometres from to Pottsville to the Queensland border.

The best of its usually long beaches is at Norries Head, where a small beach, known locally as Caba, sits between the base of the headland and the strip of wave-washed rock platform and boulders that links it to the local community of Cabarita. This is a little gem of north-facing calmer waters wedged between the rocks and backed by a fringe of shady casuarinas, a grassy park and picnic area – all a stone's throw from the main Tweed Coast road.

The beach is usually wide and sandy at high tide, dropping into deeper water filled with the rock reefs that link the adjoining headlands. Occasionally, a pulse of sand moves round the head, covering the reef with a shallow sandbar and producing a good right-hand surf break.

This is a great place to picnic, sunbake, swim in the usually mild surf and explore the rock platforms. A roving patrol from the nearby Cabarita Surf Life Saving Club keeps an eye on the beach during summer. If the summer nor'easter springs up, it's just a short stroll to the shelter of the southern Bogangar beach. Bogangar means 'place of many pippies', thanks to the edible pippies that live in the wet sand.

A track leads up onto Norries Head, which offers spectacular views north and south. No surprise that this is a popular vantage point for whale-watchers during the winter migrations. Steep sloping rocks, including deep gullies on its southern side that are fun to explore, surround the 30-metre-high grassy crest.

The small beach at Norries Head, known to the locals as 'Caba', is a little gem of north-facing waters backed by shady casuarinas. The protruding headland offers views along the coast in both directions and is popular with whale-watchers during the winter migrations.

OCEAN BEACH STRAHAN, TASMANIA

Ocean Beach, at Strahan on the wild west coast of Tasmania, is the highest energy beach in Australia and has recorded the country's biggest waves, averaging 3 metres. The biggest recorded wave here was over 21 metres. With its dangerous rips and sweeps, this is a beach to admire, *not* to swim at.

Ocean Beach at Strahan, on the untamed, rugged west coast of Tasmania, receives the full force of the wind and waves from the mighty Southern Ocean. This is the highest energy beach in Australia. Everyday waves average 3 metres and can reach up to 5 metres, but the highest wave recorded here was over 21 metres!

The beach has a fetch (the area of ocean for waves to develop) that extends 15 000 kilometres to South America – the longest in the world. Across this vast expanse the high-latitude winds – the famous roaring 40s, raging 50s and screaming 60s – stir up the ocean, sending giant waves towards this lonely bit of coast.

It's no wonder there is little here apart from the beach. The road from the historic fishing village of Strahan reaches the southern end, where there is a car park in the windswept foredunes, but the rest is just nature in the wild. On a typical day, you will see lines of breakers extending more than 500 metres out to sea, as wave after wave expends its energy across the wide surf zone of this 32-kilometre-long beach. At the shore, notice the water level suddenly rise across the flat beach then fall, exposing the wide wet sand, as a phenomenon known as 'surf beat' pumps long waves up and down the beach. This is a wild beach of very dangerous rips and sweeps. Come and admire it – but *don't* swim in it.

At the southern end of the beach, you can see the infamous 'Hells Gate', the 300-metre-wide mouth of Macquarie Harbour. It was named, in part, because of the treacherous tides and currents that race through the harbour entrance making passage by boat extremely hazardous. But the name also refers to the days when convicts en route to Australia's most dreaded penal settlement Sarah Island, passed through here in the 1820s.

BIGGEST WAVES

Southern Australia is exposed to the Southern Ocean, which produces the world's biggest waves. At the coast, the waves are recorded by wave-rider buoys, which show that the biggest *average* waves are at:

» Ocean Beach, TAS – 3 m
» Gunyah Beach, SA – 2.5 m
» Portsea Back Beach, VIC – 2.2 m

The biggest readily accessible waves to be surfed in Australian history are:

» Fairy Bower, off Manly, NSW
» Two Mile Reef, off Port Campbell, VIC
» Shipstern Bluff, TAS
» Cowaramup Bombie, off Margaret River, WA

Some waves at Cowaramup Bombie have been recorded at up to 15 m or some 5 stories high!

PALM COVE CAIRNS, QUEENSLAND

LOW WAVES | TROPICAL WATERS | BEACH GAMES | COCONUT PALMS | NIGHTLIFE

Just under half an hour north of Cairns by road lies its most famous beach – a 6-kilometre stretch of gently curving sand that holds three separate beach communities: Palm Cove, Clifton Beach and Kewarra.

Palm Cove, at the northern end, looks out towards Double Island. This is a resort-based beach with many smart beachside restaurants and bars, all in a village atmosphere with everything within walking distance. Historically, this beach, previously known as Palm Beach, was a seaside escape for farmers from the Atherton tablelands and locals from Cairns, but now its wide range of accommodation draws visitors from everywhere.

It is home to the Cairns Surf Life Saving Club, which was founded in 1924 and whose members patrol the entire beach during summer. Lifeguards and a stinger net operate seasonally. At high tide, the soft beach sand slopes into deep water but the receding tide reveals a 50-metre-wide shallow bar. Waves are usually low so this is a great beach for children and beach games. An esplanade runs the length of this kilometre-long section providing a shady walk under the coconut trees.

Halfway down the beach is the more residential area of Clifton Beach, which also has lifeguards and a stinger enclosure during the summer season. It is frequented more by locals looking for a low-key beach experience.

A small, usually closed tidal creek separates Clifton from Kewarra, in the southern corner where the beach curves round to the north in the shelter of Taylor Point. Another small tidal creek crosses the sand here and the beach becomes shallow in the southern corner where the shoals are exposed at low tide.

Despite its popularity with tourists, the entire beach retains a natural feel, with swaying palm trees and tall century-old paperbark trees lining the shore and screening the developments.

Just north of Cairns, Palm Cove in Queensland's tropical north retains a natural feel despite its popularity with tourists. Resort and restaurant developments are hidden from the beach by its fringe of coconut palms and paperbark trees.

PEACEFUL BAY WESTERN AUSTRALIA

QUAINT VILLAGE | NATIONAL PARK | FISHING | REEF DIVING | WILDFLOWERS | WALKS

Peaceful Bay, as the name implies, is a quiet, calm bay on a coast dominated by some thundering, energetic beaches. Tucked in the lee of Point Irwin, the bay faces east with its back to the prevailing westerly winds. It is further sheltered by a series of gneiss rock reefs that partly block the 400-metre-wide bay entrance.

The wide low-gradient sandy beach curves for 600 metres between the two low boundary points that are tied to the reefs. The curving shore usually has low waves or calm conditions.

This is an ideal location for those seeking a sheltered beach and a varied location for swimming, fishing (beach, inlet, rock and deep sea), snorkelling, sand boarding, sailboarding, diving the reefs or launching boats. The hundred-strong small community of Peaceful Bay is set back from the beach, with a sheltered caravan park, general store and camping area nestled among the trees. Four neat rows of original beach shacks provide an authentic flavour to this small holiday fishing community.

There is plenty to see and do in the surrounding area. The bay is partly surrounded by Walpole–Nornalup National Park which includes some 4WD tracks, raw surfing beaches at the magnificent Conspicuous Cliff and Rame Head, rock and beach fishing, crabbing in nearby Irwin Inlet, bush and coastal walks, the Valley of the Giants Treetop Walk and, in season, abundant wildflowers and bird life.

The meandering inlets around the national park, Walpole and Nornalup, according to explorer William Clark in 1841, were 'the most romantic scenery I ever witnessed in the other quarters of the globe.'

The small holiday fishing community of Peaceful Bay offers a quiet retreat on a coast dominated by thundering, energetic beaches. The meandering inlets of the Walpole-Nornalup National Park offer beautiful scenery, walks, fishing and crabbing.

PERLUBIE BEACH SOUTH AUSTRALIA

LOW-TIDE WALK TO ISLAND CONSERVATION PARK | DUNES | SEA BIRDS | KELP | SUNSETS

A round the coastline, beaches have been the site for everything from aircraft landing strips to weddings, rock concerts and land speed records, even the unexpected landing place for space junk.

Here at Perlubie, it was horse racing – on a very firm track (depending on the tide of course). This is just one example of how some remote coastal farming communities had fun, and a flutter. The local Perlubie Beach Race Day was the Melbourne Cup of the beach until it was discontinued in 1992.

Perlubie Beach, or Perlubie Landing from its wheat-shipping days, lies just off the Flinders Highway 15 kilometres north of Streaky Bay, the regional centre. This is usually a calm beach fronted by shallow sand flats that extend into Streaky Bay. Over the summer holiday period, however, it comes alive as a camping and recreation destination for the district's farming families, culminating in the famous New Year's Day Athletics Day.

Most of the year, however, you will find a curving sandy beach ideal for picnics, a beach walk, a swim in the calm bay or watching the sunset. You can also explore the backing bare sand dunes from which Perlubie derives its name, which means 'white sand hill' in the local Aboriginal language. At low tide you can walk across the sand flats to reach the southern Eba

Island Conservation Park, a significant seabird-breeding colony.

Explorer Matthew Flinders, who sailed along this coast in 1802, assumed that the 'streaked' appearance of the seas here was due to the out-flowing of a river. He was mistaken. The banded appearance is due to marine oils given off by the kelp that grows within the bays here.

CAUTION
EXCESSIVE
TIDAL
MOVEMENT
SOFT · SAND

The shallow sand flats that extend out
from Perlubie Beach into Streaky Bay
gain their banded appearance from
the oils given off by the kelp growing
abundantly in these waters. At low tide,
visitors can walk across the flats to
the Eba Island Conservation Park, an
important breeding colony for seabirds.

PIRATES BAY TASMANIA

CLIFFS | TESSELLATED PAVEMENT | CAVES | SHIPWRECKS | BLOWHOLE | CONVICT HISTORY

It's hard to believe that this beach is just an hour from Tasmania's capital. It feels so isolated and it has one of the most dramatic and beautiful coastal landscapes in Australia. But despite the name, the closest you will come to pirates here is exploring one of the scattered shipwrecks that lie at rest in this superb marine environment. The spectacular water scenery extends to the sun-filtered depths, making this a visual paradise, both above and below the surface.

The beach lies in a 2-kilometre-wide semi-circular bay, with a safe anchorage and jetty in the southern corner. Boat tours leave from here to show visitors the spectacular rocky coast, including massive cliff formations that reach 300 metres, Australia's highest. The bordering headlands also include the Tasman's Arch, the Devils Kitchen and the famous Tessellated Pavement. There is a diving school for the adventurous who want to explore, up close, the chasms, caves, wild kelp beds and extraordinary marine life.

Waves and surfing dominate the centre of the bay where the Blowhole Road provides access to the beach at several places. At the southern end is the small community of Doo Town where every house as a 'doo' in its name. including *Gunadoo, Doodle Doo, Love Me Doo, Doo Nix, Xanadu* and the little house which reputedly started the trend, the aptly labelled *Doo Little*.

While historic Pirates Bay was never the haunt of real pirates, it was host to hundreds of criminal types as a penal settlement. As a consequence it ranks as one of Australia's most infamous beaches. The northern section of the beach narrows to 100 metres at Eaglehawk Neck and in the 1830s this narrow isthmus became one of the most effective natural prison gates in the world. The isthmus was guarded by ferocious, barking dogs chained to posts at the narrowest point, designed to deter convicts escaping from nearby Port Arthur.

Today the guard post is a museum, the dogs are remembered in a snarling bronze statue and Port Arthur is a major tourist attraction. The bay is the haunt of beachgoers, surfers, bushwalkers, fisher folk, scuba divers and photographers.

The spectacular rocky coast around Pirates Bay features Australia's highest marine cliffs as well as caves, chasms, a blowhole and the famous tessellated pavement. Divers can explore the underwater rock formations and scattered shipwrecks.

BLOWHOLES & CAVES

If you are feeling a bit adventurous and want to wander around the rocks try:

» Pirates Bay, TAS – the Tasman Arch, a huge hole called the Devils Kitchen and the famous Tessellated Pavement
» Kiama, NSW – blowhole
» Quobba, WA – blowhole
» Albany, WA – the Natural Bridge

Keep an eye on the tides if you're exploring rocks at the end of a headland and always watch your footing, especially at steep drop offs.

PONDALOWIE BAY
YORKE PENINSULA, SOUTH AUSTRALIA

SEAGRASS MEADOWS | FISHING | DIVING | NATIONAL PARK | WALKS | SEALING HISTORY

The arid coast around Pondalowie Bay features stunning calcarenite headlands and lookouts. Located in the Innes National Park at the southern tip of the Yorke Peninsula, Pondalowie is popular for fishing, camping, snorkelling, wind surfing and sea kayaking.

To the local Aboriginal people, Pondalowie means 'limestone water hole' and it was the availability of fresh water on this arid coast and the bay's sheltered position, that resulted in the area's early occupation by ex-convict sealers.

Pondalowie Bay is located in the 9500-hectare Innes National Park at the southern tip of the Yorke Peninsula, with Spencer Gulf to the west and Gulf St Vincent to the east. This sparsely inhabited tip sits north of Kangaroo Island and is separated from it by Investigator Strait.

The bay opens through a 1.3-kilometre-wide gap between Middle Island and South Islet, and its shoreline is a long, curving sandy beach. The southern section of the bay is sheltered by the islet and provides an anchorage for fishing and recreational boats with seagrass growing to the shore. This is a favourite area for boat launching, beach fishers and families. Two campsites 'Casuarina' and 'Pondalowie Bay' and a few fisher shacks are located nearby. As you move up the bay, wave height increases and it becomes popular with surfers. The bay is also used for wind and kite surfing, sea kayaking, canoeing, snorkelling and scuba diving. All three camping areas shelter behind extensive coastal dunes, so you need to walk through the dunes to the beach. There is also a caravan park and tavern in nearby Marion Bay.

The surrounding area has some stunning calcarenite headlands and lookouts up to 60 metres high, including West Cape lighthouse, The Gap and Howling Cave Beach. Small Ethel Beach contains the visible remains of the wrecked *Ethel*.

There are also a number of more remote surfing spots on either side of the bay that are well worth finding. The park offers more than 50 kilometres of coastal, dune and inland walking tracks, and is some of the best coastal desert-style wilderness around.

PORT NOARLUNGA
ADELAIDE, SOUTH AUSTRALIA

SHELTERED CITY BEACH | REEFS | SNORKELLING | DIVING TRAIL | JETTY | AQUATIC RESERVE

Once a small port village, Port Noarlunga is now part of the southern suburbs of Adelaide. A marked self-guided diving trail over the shallow reefs makes this a popular place for snorkelling and scuba diving.

Port Noarlunga, on Gulf St Vincent, began life as a small coastal port. Today it is part of outer Adelaide and a popular residential and holiday resort destination just 30 kilometres south of the CBD. This is a quieter alternative to Adelaide's busier city beaches.

The original 'port' was supposed to be built on the Onkaparinga River, which enters the gulf at the southern end of the beach. But that proved too shallow so, in 1855, a jetty was constructed in waters protected by a reef that lies parallel to the shore just a few hundred metres off the northern end of the beach. The present 300-metre-long jetty dates from 1921.

The northern half of the beach lies in the lee of the reef – a naturally cemented remnant of a 100 000-year-old former beach system. This provides shelter for the beach and helps create the usually calm conditions. Eroding deep red bluffs and a foreshore reserve back the beach. The Port Noarlunga Surf Life Saving Club and kiosk are located towards the southern end near the popular jetty.

North of the jetty is Onkaparinga Aquatic Reserve – the first of its kind in South Australia. This area of shallow reefs extends out from the beach and features a marked underwater 'self-guided diving trail' that makes it a favourite scuba dive site. Divers can follow the trail, which consists of twelve glass plaques displaying features of the reef ecosystem.

South of the reef the beach continues for another kilometre to the small river mouth that flows out against the southern bluffs. This section, patrolled by the South Port Surf Life Saving Club, is more exposed and receives any swell that makes its way up the gulf producing, at times, reasonable surf.

Wheat harvesting, early 1840's

Opening of new Jetty, 1921
Image courtesy of the State Library of South Australia

Opening of new Jetty, 1921
Image courtesy of the State Library of South Australia

LONGEST BEACH JETTY

Some beaches are fronted by shallow water requiring long jetties to reach deeper water for shipping. The longest four in Australia are found at:

» Lucinda, QLD – 5.76 km, longest in southern hemisphere
» Dalrymple Bay–Hay Point, QLD – 3.8 km
» Busselton, WA – 1.8 km, longest wooden jetty in southern hemisphere
» Beachport, SA – 750 m

Busselton and Beachport jetties are open to the public. South Australia has 73 beach jetties, more than any other state. While most jetties and piers in Australia were built for landing passengers and supplies, many were used purely for promenade and pleasure.

PORTSEA MORNINGTON PENINSULA, VICTORIA

WILD SEAS | DANGEROUS SURF | BIG RIPS | HIGH DUNES | STRONG WINDS

The pounding surf and big rips at Portsea's Back Beach make it suitable for experienced surfers only. This wild and spectacular coast is popular with Melbourne's well-to-do, though cautious swimmers would be advised to stick to Portsea's Front Beach on the calm waters of Port Phillip Bay.

Portsea on the Mornington Peninsula has two faces. The front or main beach sits on the placid waters of Port Phillip Bay. The residential area behind the beach, where many of the streets are lined with majestic, mature pine trees, is an enclave for Melbourne's well-to-do.

In stark contrast to the tranquil, ordered main beach, the Back Beach 2 kilometres to the south is Australia's highest energy and most hazardous patrolled beach. The waves and wind delivered the sand that built the high dunes behind the beach. The waves have also swept much of the sand from the water up onto the beach, leaving behind a reef-littered surf zone. This combination of consistently high waves and reefs produces a dangerous mix of strong currents and permanent seaward-flowing rip currents.

In 1967, just 4 kilometres to the west at Cheviot Beach, the then prime minister and skin diver, Harold Holt, went for a quick dip and was never seen again. Many conspiracy theories were put forward but the bold-hearted prime minister was, in fact, swimming on a very dangerous rip-dominated part of the coast.

The only structure on this section of coast is the Portsea Surf Life Saving Club, which dates back to 1949, and whose members are vigilant in their efforts to maintain the safety of swimmers and surfers. Despite its dangerous character, the Back Beach is very popular during summer and when waves are lower. There are four large dune-top car parks with ramps leading down to the beach. Bring everything you need to the beach because it's a steep walk back. Apart from the surf club kiosk, there is nothing else on offer, other than waves, surf and wild rips, though, when conditions are right, there are some fine surfing waves.

If you are venturing down to the beach and entering the water make sure it is patrolled and swim only close to shore and between the patrol flags. Be warned, there are always strong rip currents along this beach so, if unsure, stick to the Front Beach.

RAINBOW BAY GOLD COAST, QUEENSLAND

Rainbow Bay on the Gold Coast is home to the 'Superbank', which lays claim to the world's longest, most perfect waves. Sand moves around the bay's southern point in pulses to produce a wide sandbar that creates excellent surfing conditions.

Listed as having one of the world's longest, most perfect waves, Rainbow Bay with its 'Superbank' is the southernmost beach on the Gold Coast.

Nestled between the basalt rocks of Greenmount and the ridged sedimentary rocks of Snapper Rocks–Point Danger, the 300-metre-long beach faces north-west, providing a setting for glorious sunsets over Greenmount. There are views through the giant pines and pandanus right up the coast to Surfers Paradise.

Sand moves around the southern point in pulses, which can produce a wide sandbar. This is where the famous waves of Snapper Rock break, a site for international surfing competitions and now a National Surfing Reserve. When extra sand was pumped round the point in the 2000s, it produced an exceptionally large sandbar and good long waves, which became known as 'Superbank'. However, it also widened the beach to such an extent the locals complained about the trek to get to the water's edge. All has now returned to normal, though natural sand pulses still affect the width of the beach and the nature of the surf.

The beach usually has a shallow sandbar extending out to where the surf breaks. Out the back, you will find long-board riders catching the long ride in from out wide, while hundreds of short boarders jostle for the inside waves in the tighter sections closer to Snapper Rocks. A shallow gutter just off the beach creates a calm patch for swimmers and gentler white water for learners. In the eastern corner, the Rainbow Bay Surf Life Saving Club occupies what must be one of the best beachfronts in Australia, rivalled only by nearby Currumbin SLSC. Make sure you take the time to have a snack or a drink on the club balcony at sunset.

For the energetic there are also coastal walks in both directions – south round Point Danger to Duranbah and north to Coolangatta via the pedestrian boardwalk to Greenmount Beach. Lookouts on both headlands offer superb views.

RAINBOW BEACH QUEENSLAND

COLOURED SANDS | BIG DUNES | CALM WATERS IN THE SOUTH | SURF IN THE NORTH

Rainbow Beach, on Queensland's Cooloola Coast, is named after the 'rainbow' of sands that are exposed along its high-scarped dune face, providing the longest and most colourful backdrop to any beach in Australia. Local Aboriginal legend has it that the coastal cliffs were given these hues when Yiningie, the spirit of the gods representing the Rainbow, was killed in a fight and spread his colourful spirits across the cliffs.

The story of the coloured sands actually goes back several hundred thousand years. Each time the sea level rose to near its present height, sand was blown onto the dunes. Over time, layer after layer of sand dune accumulated until it reached the present towering height. After each major accumulation, vegetation and soil slowly formed on the dune surface, colouring the sand – until it,

too, was buried by the next layer of sand 100 000 years later. When the most recent sea level rise reached its present position, it not only created the curving bay but also scarped the dunes, exposing these layers of different coloured soils.

The present beach begins at Inskip Point, opposite Fraser Island, and heads south for 10 kilometres to the township of Rainbow Bay. Then the scarped coloured sands continue for another 8 kilometres before the beach finally curves round to face west in the lee of Double Island Point. Waves range from very low here to more than 1 metre at the town, where you'll find the surf life saving club, and up to 1.5 m at Inskip Point. Surf and rip currents dominate much of the beach, however, so swim only in the patrolled area.

The coloured sands in the dunes of Rainbow Beach are a record of past dune heights and long-vanished vegetation. Local Aboriginal legend has it that the coastal cliffs were given these hues when Yiningie, the spirit of the gods representing the Rainbow, was killed in a fight and spread his colourful spirits across the sand.

REDBILL–DIAMOND ISLAND
TASMANIA

LOW-TIDE WALK TO ISLAND | FAIRY PENGUINS | BIRD LIFE | SURFING | FISHING PORT

Pied oystercatchers, with their red bills, hooded plovers and fairy penguins are all residents of Redbill Beach, located just north of the popular coastal town of Bicheno. It's a great beach for a picnic, swim, surf, walk or just to enjoy nature's variety.

Bicheno started out as a whaling settlement and is still a fishing port. The fishing fleet is based in The Gulch in the lee of granitic, wave-washed Governor Island. The sloping granite coast extends north of the town to Redbill Beach, whose sandy shore curves northward for 1 kilometre until it reaches Diamond Island, which is connected to the mainland by a low strip of exposed sand known as a tombolo. The beach is composed of pure white sand backed by a low grassy foredune, then green slopes rising to the road behind. It is partly sheltered by the island at

the northern end and in the south by a headland, although a sign at the southern end warns about the rip that runs out along the rocks. There is higher surf, and rip currents, in the more exposed centre. Although the beach is located just off the east-coast highway, the only public access is from the southern headland or by following the coastal walkway from Bicheno.

This is a great beach for walking. At low tide and when the waves are low you can walk out along the tombolo to the island, a huge lump of wave-smoothed granite topped with sparse vegetation that is now a nature reserve. During the spring–summer breeding season you can watch the fairy penguins returning home at dusk to their burrows both on the island and in the foredune. Hooded plovers and oystercatchers are a common sight along the edge of the shoreline.

Redbill Beach is connected to the offshore Diamond Island by a low strip of sand known as a tombolo, which visitors can walk across at low tide. The island's nature reserve is home to a host of birds including fairy penguins.

REFUGE COVE
WILSONS PROMONTORY, VICTORIA

NATIONAL PARK | WALK-IN CAMPING | DEEP WATERS | DENSE FORESTS | ABORIGINAL MIDDENS

Wilsons Promontory, commonly known as the 'Prom', contains 50 000 hectares of raw coastal wilderness on mainland Australia's southernmost tip. It is one of Victoria's oldest and most popular national parks.

Tranquil Refuge Cove, on the remote eastern shore, has provided shelter to humans for thousands of years. Indigenous Australians fished its waters and left rich shell middens on the shore. Later, from the 1830s, a whaling station operated here, followed by a granite quarry and timber-getting operations and during WWII commandos were trained here.

Since then tranquillity has returned, with only passing fishing boats and sailing craft finding shelter in the cove, including some yachts that have retreated here after suffering damage during the annual Sydney to Hobart race.

Getting here by land is a pilgrimage of sorts. It's a 15-kilometre trek across Wilsons Promontory from Tidal River to this cove, where most hikers, and sailors, head for the more sheltered southern beach, a 150-metre-long strip of north-facing sand, edging the crystal clear waters. There is a great camping area here with a small creek hard against the end of the beach.

If you arrive by water, you will pass through the cove's 300-metre-wide entrance bordered by steeply rising forested granite slopes. The cove opens to an elongated, wide bay with two small beaches and deep, protected waters that extend to the shore. The remainder of the shoreline is covered in dense eucalyptus forest that runs right down to the water.

Refuge Cove will allow you to experience the natural beauty of Wilsons Promontory away from the bustle of Tidal River (see Tidal River), but, you need to be a well-equipped hiker or sailor to make the trip.

With the only access by foot or boat, Wilsons Promontory's Refuge Cove remains a peaceful retreat. Hikers who venture on the 15-kilometre trek from Tidal River can camp beside a small creek at one end of the beach.

RESORT BEACH LIZARD ISLAND, QUEENSLAND

GREAT BARRIER REEF | SNORKELLING | WILDLIFE | WHALES | PRISTINE ENVIRONMENT

Rising out of the deep blue Coral Sea some 250 kilometres north of Cairns, Lizard Island is a reef-fringed high granite island blessed with 20 beaches. The entire island is a national park and the surrounding waters are part of the Great Barrier Reef Marine Park. This pristine beach environment is accessible only by plane or boat.

The first European visitor was explorer James Cook who, trapped within a labyrinth of coral reefs in 1770, landed on the island after his encounter with Endeavour Reef. Cook and his party climbed to the island's summit ('Cooks Look') in a bid to find a way out. He named the island after the many tunnelling lizards he came across.

The only development on the island is a resort, airport and the Australian Museum's

marine research station. The resort faces north onto the white sands of Resort Beach, fringed by granite headlands and a small island off the western end, with coral reefs growing to within a few metres of the shore. Fringing reefs encircle the island and, on the southern side, enclose the fabulous Blue Lagoon, a snorkeller's and diver's paradise of colourful tropical fish and magnificent corals. You are likely to come face to face with lizards, turtles, manta rays, rare birds, butterflies and hundreds of other amazing creatures. Take the time to explore the island on foot to find your own 'private' beach, or enjoy the view from Cooks Look, which is a great vantage point when migrating whales pass by. You can also tour the world famous research station and learn how scientists are unravelling the secrets of the Great Barrier Reef.

The high granite outcrop of Lizard Island is surrounded by the corals of the Great Barrier Reef and offers superb snorkelling and other wildlife encounters. Visitors are likely to come face to face with lizards, turtles, manta rays, rare birds, butterflies and hundreds of other creatures.

161

COASTAL DRIVES

Only a few highways actually hug the coast and those providing the best views and access are:

» The Cook Highway, Cairns–Mossman, QLD
» Lawrence Hargrave Drive–Sea Cliff Bridge, NSW
» The Great Ocean Road, VIC
» Esperance Coastal Drive, WA
» Indian Ocean Drive, WA

Australian coastal drives enable you to experience and view spectacular sections of coast from the comfort of your car.

SANDY CAPE WESTERN AUSTRALIA

MARINE PARK | SEA STACKS | CRAWL-THROUGH CAVE | REEFED LAGOON | SNORKELLING

The magnificent Indian Ocean Drive, which opened in 2010, links the coastal communities of Lancelin, Cervantes, Jurien Bay and Green Head. This region is known as the Turquoise Coast, named after the colour of the water as it reflects off the white carbonate sands of the sea floor.

There are some 100 beaches along the drive, although many are only accessible on foot or by 4WD. The pick of them all is Sandy Cape, 15 kilometres north of Jurien Bay.

The beach and the cape – a dune-draped headland that forms the southern boundary of the curving beach – are now part of the Sandy Cape Recreational Park. The beach has long been a local favourite but it was not always so pristine. Grain was shipped from this region in the 1880s and then fishing shacks appeared from the 1920s. Eventually all of the shacks were removed and the park was declared in 2000. Today the public can enjoy this beautiful site either on daytrips or by camping.

There is plenty to enjoy here. At the beach, a walking ramp leads to a bluff-top lookout on the prominent southern headland. A little further north, there are some calcarenite sea stacks, including one with a crawl-through cave. Further on again, a bare sand dune spills down onto the beach and is a favourite place to climb and slide for the young and young at heart. The beach keeps curving gently to the north, where the reefs that extend north of the head create a sheltered lagoon.

Most people come here to camp, fish, swim and snorkel. The more adventurous try scuba diving, or walk to the southern side of the headland where there is a small rip-crossed surf beach. You can also launch boats off the beach as vehicles are allowed to drive and park on a section of the beach between the high and low water marks.

Nearby are the world-famous Pinnacles in Nambung National Park, eroded remnants of a limestone bed. Offshore is Jurien Bay Marine Park and to the north is the start of Western Australia's Coral Coast.

Sandy Cape is the pick of the beaches along the magnificent new Indian Ocean Drive that has opened up Western Australia's turquoise coast. Its white sands and sheltered lagoon make this a popular destination for divers and snorkellers.

SEAL ROCKS NEW SOUTH WALES.

NATIONAL PARK | BIG DUNES | SEA CAVES | FUR-SEALS | HISTORIC LIGHTHOUSE

Seal Rocks is named after a series of steep rocky outcrops located 2 kilometres off Sugarloaf Point where Australian fur-seals haul out to sunbake during the summer months. The tall lighthouse on the point was built in 1875 to warn shipping of the projecting point and the hazardous reefs, although there have been some shipwrecks since. The sheltered northern side of the point houses a small historic timber and fishing settlement, now surrounded by Myall Lakes National Park and the Port Stephens–Great Lakes Marine Park.

Four picturesque beaches border Sugarloaf Point. On the northern, sheltered side is Number One, the first beach you see when arriving by car and the most popular, offering lower waves and some surf on the point. It is also has a camping and caravan area in the backing valley. Next is Boat Beach where fishing and dive boats haul up on the beach and modest houses line the backing slopes. Further on, you reach the lighthouse car park and from here it is just a short walk to the lighthouse, via some spectacular sea caves. The view along the beach from this rugged point is one of the best on the east coast. Just beyond the point is Lighthouse Beach, which is fully exposed to southerly waves and is normally cut by strong rip channels and currents. Its southern neighbour, and near twin, is Treachery Beach, used mainly by seasoned surfers and fishers who camp in the large camping area behind the dunes. Both beaches are, however, treacherous and swimming is not advised.

This protruding point on the coast marks the point where the warm East Australian Current is deflected offshore into a series of eddies and where the tropical waters from the north transform to more temperate conditions and associated marine ecosystems.

Seal Rocks is also where the southerly winds have built the largest and highest sand dunes in New South Wales, reaching 160 metres in height and now covered by dense vegetation. If looking for bare sand dunes head a few kilometres south to Mungo Brush and Dark Point. These dunes are backed by the magnificent Myall Lakes, the largest coastal lake system in New South Wales.

The rocky outcrops of Seal Rocks extend out to sea off Sugarloaf Point, separating quiet Boat Beach (top right), home to the small Seal Rocks community, from the more exposed Lighthouse Beach (bottom and top left).

SECOND VALLEY
FLEURIEU PENINSULA, SOUTH AUSTRALIA

HISTORIC HAMLET | JETTY | COLOURFUL ROCKS | SNORKELLING | LEAFY SEA DRAGONS

Charming Second Valley is a small farming and fishing hamlet on the shores of Gulf St Vincent, with a permanent population of around 200. It has a 'lost in time' seaside setting much admired by visitors.

Just 90 kilometres south of Adelaide on the Fleurieu Peninsula this quaint haven includes two small communities in the secluded valley.

There is a 150-year-old restored grain mill on the main road, while the main cluster of heritage cottages sits behind a narrow gap in the valley sides.

The shorefront car park leads to a pocket of sand bordered at its southern end by an old stone and timber fishing jetty. The clear inviting waters around the jetty make this a popular spot for

divers and underwater photographers. If you climb the jetty you'll see a second small gravel beach where the old boat sheds once stood. That path is worth exploring if only to study the psychedelic mosaic of geological rock swirls.

It is usually calm here and the water offers great swimming, kayaking, snorkelling and diving. The wonderfully diverse marine life includes the enchanting leafy sea dragon, South Australia's official marine emblem. The area around here plays host to the annual Leafy Sea Dragon Festival.

Second Valley is also on the way to historic Rapid Bay, the Deep Creek Conservation Park, which faces Backstairs Passage and Cape Jervis, the ferry terminal for Kangaroo Island.

The clear waters around the historic jetty at Second Valley, on South Australia's Fleurieu Peninsula, are home to leafy sea dragons and a host of other marine life, making this a popular destination for divers and underwater photographers.

SECRET BEACH MALLACOOTA, VICTORIA

JAGGED ROCKS | SEA CAVE | PRISTINE ENVIRONMENT | MODERATE SURF | NATIONAL PARK

This beach is hidden away adjacent to the Croajingolong National Park, a coastal wilderness near the NSW–Victorian border. It's one of those 'just off the highway' gems.

Twenty-five kilometres off the Princes Highway from Genoa, the fishing village of Mallacoota sits on the shores of the superb Mallacoota Inlet. Croajingolong National Park encloses Mallacoota in a World Biosphere Reserve, so the area is special in many ways.

If you follow the coast road that runs south from the village for 6 kilometres, just past the airport you'll find a bluff-top car park and a walking track that descends through a forested gully to this pristine 200-metre-long – 'secret' beach. The sands are bordered by jagged colourful rock composed of contorted sandstone and shale, with rock reefs extending off both small headlands. The northern headland has been eroded, forming a sea cave that is accessible at low tide. Waves are usually low to moderate and break over a sand bar that is often cut by one or two rip channels. These waves offer the chance for some surfing, but be careful if swimming. During bigger seas, bull kelp is torn off the rock reefs and washes ashore. At the back of the beach there is a low grassy foredune, then a valley bordered by densely vegetated bluffs and headlands.

This is a great place to come if you like getting off the beaten track to discover a beautiful natural section of coast for surfing, sightseeing, canoeing, fishing or sunbaking. If you want to explore further, the road continues for a few kilometres to the small Shipwreck Creek camping and picnic area inside the national park.

Secret Beach is hidden away next to the Croajingalong National Park, just outside the coastal town of Mallacoota. Erosion of the northern headland has formed a sea cave that is accessible at low tide.

SEVEN MILE BEACH
SHOALHAVEN, NEW SOUTH WALES

FINE SANDS | NATIONAL PARK | COASTAL FOREST | SEA EAGLES | AVIATION HISTORY

The fine sands of Seven Mile Beach south of Sydney create such a firm surface that the beach was used as a runway by pioneering aviator Charles Kingsford-Smith in 1933. The eucalyptus forests behind the beach are part of the Seven Mile Beach National Park, which is home to a rich variety of bird life including the white-breasted sea eagle.

Seven Mile beach is the longest beach on the New South Wales coast south of Sydney and also the one with the finest sand, which has created in a hard, firm surface.

Pioneering aviator Charles Kingsford-Smith took advantage of this when he used the beach as a runway on his historic first commercial Trans-Tasman flight to New Zealand in 1933. A small park on the northern headland commemorates this feat as well as providing sweeping views down the beach.

The beach stretches for 12.5 kilometres (7.5 miles) to the usually blocked Shoalhaven River mouth and continues for another 5 kilometres along neighbouring Comerong Island. The waves combine with the fine sand to maintain a wide, double-bar surf zone, with rip currents common along this exposed beach.

Basaltic Black Head, now largely covered by the houses of Gerroa, dominates the northern end and is linked to the beach by a footbridge across the small mangrove-lined Crooked River. There

is a wide rock platform around the base of the head and a rock reef providing some shelter to the northern corner of the beach. In the south is the historic community of Shoalhaven Heads, settled in the 1830s when it was known as Jerry Bailey. Seven Mile Beach National Park, which occupies much of the area between the two heads, preserves a rich littoral eucalyptus ecosystem that sits atop a series of former beaches. There is a wide range of bird life here, including the white-breasted sea eagle.

Forested Mount Coolangatta ('splendid view' in the local Aboriginal language) forms a towering 320-metre backdrop to the beach. In 1822, it became the site of the first European settlement in the Illawarra and its buildings are now part of the Coolangatta Estate resort.

Despite its long history, Seven Mile remains relatively undeveloped and with the protection of the national park it will stay that way – but with good access and facilities at either end including the Shoalhaven Heads Surf Life Saving Club.

RISK WA
Attent
Divers, Jumpers, Climbers
Children and Membe
During Jumping, climbing of
of Brs Bridge is DANGER

RISKS INCLU

SEVENTY FIVE MILE BEACH
FRASER ISLAND, QUEENSLAND

ANCIENT COLOURED DUNES | FRESHWATER LAKES | RAINFOREST | WORLD HERITAGE AREA

Fraser Island is the world's largest sand island, site of Queensland's longest beach and home to ancient coloured sand dunes. It has bubbling freshwater springs, pure-bred dingoes, rainforest-covered dunes and pristine freshwater lakes high in the dunes, including the world's largest. It's also a national park and World Heritage Area.

Aboriginal people call this place K'gari ... 'paradise'. It was named Fraser Island after Eliza Fraser, the sole survivor of an 1836 shipwreck who lived with local Aboriginal people before being rescued.

Beaches ring the entire 200 kilometres of the island's shore but the best by far is the long, straight Seventy Five Mile Beach. Fully exposed to the prevailing southerly swell, the beach offers a long, wide surf zone, with rip channels regularly spaced along the shore. It's great for beach fishing but be cautious if swimming. Other beach highlights include the bubbling Champagne Pools, Indian Head (from where you can often

see the sharks in the surf), the rusty wreck of the *Maheno* and Ely Creek which is capable of delivering four million litres of clear fresh water to the beach every hour. Pure and clear, the creek has its own distinctive and varied wildlife. For a memorable experience, make sure you wander along the boardwalk and float down this forested creek in the cool shallows.

Fraser is also a bird watcher's paradise, with an incredible 354 species seen here. In the ocean, marine life includes dolphins, whales, dugongs (on the lee side), turtles, huge rays and tailor, the fishers' favourite.

To get to Fraser Island, take the vehicular ferry from Inskip Point (see Rainbow Beach) for the short trip to the southern tip of the island. If driving, make sure you know how to handle a 4WD on a wave-washed beach and watch out for the rising tide and soft sand around the freshwater springs. There are three resorts on the island, as well as holiday cabins and formal camping areas.

This long beach on Queensland's Fraser Island boasts ancient coloured dunes, bubbling freshwater springs, pristine lakes, and rainforest filled with wildlife. An astonishing 354 species of birds have been seen on the island, while the surrounding waters are home to dolphins, whales, dugongs, turtles and huge rays.

AUSTRALIA'S ONLY PURE SHELL BEACH | HIGH SALINITY | WORLD HERITAGE AREA

The shoreline here is composed entirely of shells – millions of them, several metres deep. It is the only beach of this type in Australia and one of only two shell beaches like it in the world.

Shell Beach is an example of the amazing environments that have evolved in the arid, high-salinity environment of Shark Bay. The beach is located deep in the bay at the base of Lharidon Bight, so far from the entrance and 'fresh' seawater that the high evaporation results in salinity reaching twice that of sea water (70 parts of salt per 1000 parts of sea water).

Because of the high salinity little can live here, but one mollusc does. In fact, it thrives as it has no predator. Scientifically known as *Fragum erugatum*, the cardiid cockle or 'coquina bivalve' is a small white bivalve that lives and thrives on the kilometre-wide shallow sand flats that ring the shore. These bivalves live and die in their millions here, and the gentle waves of the bight wash them ashore intact where they have slowly built this unique beach.

So many shells have collected here over the past few thousand years that the beach has built out 200 metres into the bay, creating a series of very low former shell beaches, known as shell ridges. Some of the older beach ridges, because of the pure calcium carbonate content, have been

naturally cemented together into shellrock, a form of limestone that has been used in local buildings.

The Denham Road runs right past the base of this curving beach and the easy access makes it a popular stop on the long drive into the World Heritage-listed Shark Bay. Take a walk out across the ridges to the beach and admire what nature can produce when you add a bit more salt to the water.

BEST SHELLS

Shells of some sort are washed up on most beaches. But if you want something special you should visit:

» Eighty Mile Beach, WA – richest and most varied collection
» Shell Beach, Shark Bay, WA – nothing *but* shells, but all of the same type

Finding special shells for souvenirs is one of the great pastimes of beach goers ... but don't take the creatures known as intertidal invertebrates or living shells!

Shell Beach on the World Heritage-listed Shark Bay is the only beach in Australia made entirely of shells – millions of them, piled several metres deep. Located deep in the bay, where the salinity is twice that of normal sea water, the shallow sand flats here are largely devoid of life but the shells are evidence of the one species of mollusc that thrives here.

SHELLEY BEACH NEW SOUTH WALES

REMOTE WALK-IN BEACH | NATIONAL PARK | BEACHSIDE CAMPING | WALKS | WILDLIFE

Remote Shelley Beach is a highlight on the stunning coastal walk through the Yuraygir National Park from Angourie to Red Cliff. The beach, which is only accessible on foot, offers the only beachside campsite along the walk.

Shelley Beach is a remote walk-in beach located in Yuraygir National Park on the New South Wales north coast. This national park contains more than 60 kilometres of coast, between Angourie and Red Rock.

This is the traditional country of the Yaegl and Gumbaynggir indigenous people whose ancestors camped, fished and held ceremonies in the region. Today the park is interspersed with a collection of small communities that occupy pockets of freehold land well off the highway.

The park contains 48 remote beaches and the best way to see them is on the coastal walk from Angourie to Red Cliff in the park's north. The half-day coastal walk starts at surf-sacred Angourie village, then runs along the intervening beaches: Back Angourie (part of the Angourie National Surfing Reserve), Little Shelley, Shelley, Shelley Head, Caves, Plumbago and Red Cliff. There is vehicle access at either end. The 10-kilometre walk takes in the intervening headlands and stretches of heathland, lagoons and swamps. The area is rich with birds, native animals, amphibians and reptiles.

Shelley is located midway along the walk and offers the only beachside campsite, on Shelley Head. The beach is just 800 metres long, curving between the southern Shelley Head and the northern One Man Bluff. Two small creeks cross the southern end of the beach and a well-vegetated foredune runs the length of the beach. The head offers a little shelter in the south but the beach is exposed and there are usually rip currents.

On Back Angourie and Plumbago, water drains from dune-covered bluffs onto the beaches forming clear freshwater pools and streams, Little Shelley has rock pools and reefs, and there are caves on the northern headland of Caves Beach. All seven beaches are exposed and offer surf for the intrepid. But take care if swimming as there are many rips on all the beaches.

MOST POPULAR NAME

The most common names for Australian beaches are:

» Shell, Shelly or Shelley – 50 around the coast

» Pebbly – 17 around the coast

But most of Australia's 11 761 beaches have no name at all.

SILICA BEACH
KIMBERLEY, WESTERN AUSTRALIA

REMOTE ISLAND BEACH | PRISTINE WATERS | WHITE SANDS | CAMPING | CROCODILES

Silica Beach is an enigma. Located on uninhabited Hidden Island, part of the Buccaneer Archipelago in the remote western Kimberley, it is a pure white beach composed of silica, on a coast dominated by beaches composed of carbonate material – shell and coral fragments. The source of the silica remains a mystery, but there is no doubt about its purity and clarity. And, when you walk on it, it is just as extraordinary to listen to, as it is to see.

Like most Kimberley beaches, this one is short, just 150 metres long. It occupies the mouth of a small valley, with ragged tree-covered sandstone bluffs rising to 20 metres on either side and two mangrove-fringed headlands extending 500 metres seaward to form a sheltered north-facing bay. Some 90 kilometres north of Derby and north-east of Cape Leveque this is as far from civilisation as many people will ever go. You can only reach the beach by boat but, with generally deep water in the bay and off the beach, particularly at high tide, boats can moor against the shore.

Despite its isolation, boats, particularly luxury cruise vessels, do visit here. It's one of the 'must see' spots on the 4000-kilometre-long Kimberley coast.

This is a great beach for a dip (but do keep an eye out for crocodiles), a picnic or an overnight camp. Make sure you take your camera and climb the headland for a great view of the rugged and beautiful Kimberley coastline.

Located on Hidden Island, part of the Kimberley's remote Buccaneer Archipelago, Silica Beach is accessible only by boat although the deep waters mean vessels can generally moor close to shore. This is a wonderful place to cool off but visitors do need to keep an eye out for crocodiles.

SMITHS BEACH

MARGARET RIVER, WESTERN AUSTRALIA

SURFING | WINE REGION | GOURMET FOODS | NATIONAL PARK | FORESTS | COASTAL WALKS

This beach is set on a 100-kilometre stretch of some of Australia's best surf, adjacent to one of the country's leading gastronomic and wine-making regions. This wild and rugged coastline with lush forested hinterland enjoys what many consider the finest consistent surfing waves anywhere on the planet.

Wave-rich Leeuwin-Naturaliste National Park runs from Yallingup in the north to Augusta at the south-west tip of Australia where the great Indian and Southern oceans meet. Among the 75 swimming and surfing beaches on this stretch of coast, wide, accessible and moderately sheltered Smiths Beach is the most popular. It nestles 2 kilometres off the main road at the base of a sloping drive down to the beach, which also leads to three beachfront resorts. The beach curves slightly north-east for 1.8 kilometres, interrupted by some intertidal and offshore reefs. The southern headland

provides some protection, with waves averaging about 1 metre in the south rising to 1.5 metres in the north, where rip currents are present. Vegetated dunes climb the backing slopes, and Gunyulgup Brook drains across the southern section of the beach.

There is plenty of consistent reef surf on the southern point and central reefs including the well-known 'Super Tubes', as well as 'Torpedo Rocks', 'Stepping Stones' and 'Palisades'. Most swimmers stay in the southern corner while surfers and the popular surf school usually head up the beach.

The famous Cape-to-Cape walking track continues along the beach and north to neighbouring Yallingup Beach. Yallingup is considered the birthplace of surfing in Western Australia and, with Kalbarri (see Kalbarri) and Margaret River is one of the three National Surfing Reserves in the state.

Famous for its 'Super Tubes', beautiful Smiths Beach in the Leeuwin-Naturaliste National Park has some of the world's finest consistent surfing waves. For non-surfers, the beach is also part of the famous Cape-to-Cape walking track and is close to the wineries and gourmet food offerings of the Margaret River region.

SNELLINGS BEACH
KANGAROO ISLAND, SOUTH AUSTRALIA

BEACH WALKS | ROCK PLATFORMS | PATTERNED ROCKS | TIDAL POOLS | FISHING

Snellings Beach, the most popular beach on Kangaroo Island's north coast, is located 60 kilometres west of Kingscote along the slow gravel North Coast road, which crosses the backing Middle River flats and skirts the western end of the beach.

There is a scattering of dwellings and not much else other than a car park and small camping area. A solitary Robinson Crusoe shack is wedged in amongst the western rocks on an otherwise natural beach.

This 600-metre-long beach faces north-west exposing it to the occasional westerly swell that makes its way along the north coast, which can at times produce moderate beach breaks for surfing. But this is really just a great beach to walk along, or for swimmers to enjoy the usually low waves.

Middle River flows down the valley behind and during winter can break out against the eastern rocks. Most of the sand on the beach has, however, come from the sea and consists of fine white carbonate particles that produce the low beach gradient and wide surf zone. At either end, the jagged, contorted rock layers form intricate patterns as they rise to high headlands with irregular rock platforms at their base. These platforms are worth exploring for the amazing rock formations and fascinating tidal pools.

Kangaroo Island's north coast has some surf but Pennington Beach on the south coast offers the most consistent surf. If you are looking for a quiet beach close to Kingscote, try Emu Bay, the locals' favourite.

A solitary fishing shack sits at one end of the otherwise natural Snellings Beach on the northern shores of Kangaroo Island. Rock platforms at the base of each headland are worth exploring for their amazing rock formations and busy tidal pools.

SOUTH BROULEE NEW SOUTH WALES

SURFING | ROCK POOLS | NATURE RESERVE | UNDEVELOPED COAST | TIDAL POOLS

The rock wall at the southern end of South Broulee was built to protect the former working port at Moruya and is now one of the few signs of development on this otherwise natural surf beach. At the northern end is the nature reserve of Broulee Island — really a headland connected to the mainland by a sandy spit — where visitors can admire the tidal pools and geological patterns on a stroll around its wide rock platforms.

Broulee is a small coastal settlement renowned for its beaches, estuaries and island. This vibrant local community, with its commitment to maintaining the beautiful coastline and natural environment, is also the focal point for surfing, surf lifesaving and surf schools in the area. There are two main beaches here, the sheltered Broulee fronting the main part of town and the more exposed and natural South Broulee.

Broulee Island, a nature reserve and sand-tied headland, forms the northern boundary of South Broulee Beach. At the other end is South Head, with its popular surf break known as 'The Wall'. The Moruya River enters the sea here and a 500-metre-long rock retaining wall, built in the 1940s when Moruya was still a working coastal port, extends out into the water.

Shipping was once important at either end of the beach – Broulee Island sheltered a port in the 1840s – but the beach itself did

not come into prominence until the advent of surfboard riding in the 1960s. It was then that travelling surfers discovered the consistent banks and breaks at South Broulee and 'The Wall', and later the big reef break at Pink Rocks out on the northern side of the island. Broulee Surfers Surf Life Saving Club was established in the northern corner of the beach in 1979 and is still the only building on the beach. The beach is exposed and there are many rips, so be sure to swim only between the flags. The main, central stretch of beach is crown land, and a dense coastal forest extends inland from here.

It is possible to drive right to the northern tip of the beach where there is also a fair weather boat ramp. While you are here, take time to explore Broulee Island. It's an easy one-hour stroll around its wide basalt rock platforms, which feature intricate joint patterns, rock pools and gullies and a littering of storm-deposited boulders and cobble ridges.

MOST POPULAR

Australia's four most popular beaches based on number of beach goers are:

» Surfers Paradise, QLD
» Bondi, NSW
» Glenelg, SA
» Cottesloe, WA

Members of the Surf Life Saving Clubs patrol all of these beaches.

SURFERS PARADISE
GOLD COAST, QUEENSLAND

MOST VISITED BEACH IN AUSTRALIA | SURFING | NIGHTLIFE | CITY BY THE SEA

'Sea Glint' was one name suggested by entrepreneur Jim Cavill in the 1930s to brand this once-sleepy settlement. But it seems the name that eventually stuck has been a commercial winner.

No other city in the world has been planned and promoted around a beach culture as much as the Gold Coast's Surfers Paradise. This formerly isolated infertile stretch of sand, originally grazed in the 1870s and left barren for years with not much more than a beach pub and an adjoining zoo, has become a beach phenomenon worth billions of dollars to the national economy.

'Surfers', like Sydney's Bondi, is famous for those icons of the beach – the lifesaver and the surfer. Both are powerful emblems of beach culture and they have been energetically promoted. The advantage Surfers Paradise has over Bondi is the length of its sand, which runs for 16 kilometres from Southport Seaway down to the Nobby–Miami headland.

This stretch of coast is home to eight surf life saving clubs and 17 lifeguard towers, a testament to its popularity and the degree of surveillance required to maintain safety on this energetic coastline. This is particularly important as many of the tourists who come here are not familiar with Australian surf conditions.

Behind the beach, there is a near-continuous grassy foreshore reserve and, at Surfers, an extensive boardwalk. Across the road from the beach stand spectacular beachfront homes, Australia's tallest residential building, hundreds of motels, hotels, holiday units, restaurants, bars and all the other amenities you would expect of a major tourist destination.

Surfers Paradise on the Gold Coast receives more visitors each year than any other beach in Australia. In recognition of its popularity with visitors, many of whom are not familiar with Australian surf conditions, the beach is home to no fewer than eight surf lifesaving clubs and 17 lifeguard towers.

TANGALOOMA MORETON ISLAND, QUEENSLAND

DOLPHINS | WHALES | SHIPWRECKS | MIDDENS | FERRY RIDE FROM BRISBANE

Moreton Island, at the entrance to Moreton Bay, is one giant mass of sand – and that means great beaches on every side. This magnificent island, now a national park, is located directly north-east of Brisbane and is a favourite day trip by ferry. The trip takes just over an hour and a day spent here is a peaceful alternative to the Gold Coast. Of the four small settlements on the bay side, Tangalooma's sheltered beach is the best.

Thought by explorer James Cook to be part of the mainland when he named the northern rocky outcrop Cape 'Morton' in 1770, the island remains the traditional land of the Morrgunpin people, with large middens attesting to their long occupation. The cape is the site of Queensland's oldest lighthouse, guiding ships into Moreton Bay and towards the port of Brisbane.

Europeans first settled the island, which is some 37 kilometres long and 13 kilometres at its widest point, in 1847. In time, Tangalooma became a busy whaling station and some evidence of that history can still be seen. By contrast, today's visitors to Tangalooma know it as a point of departure for whale-watching tours, just one of the many things to do here. The small community has a wide range of accommodation as well as camping areas beside clear creeks and lagoons. There are walking trails through the coastal heath and, just off the beach, a string of half-sunken shipwrecks attracts snorkellers and divers. Inland, two lofty sandhills, Mount Tempest (280 metres) and Storm Mountain (264 metres) are the highest, vegetated coastal sandhills in the world.

Over on the island's exposed east coast there is a long stretch of beach breaks. The surf here might look inviting but swimmers should be aware that it is unpatrolled and hazardous.

BIGGEST SAND DUNES

Australia has some impressive sand dunes, including a world record:

» Fraser Island, QLD – world's biggest single coastal sand dune, 125 m long and up to 20 km wide
» Moreton Island, QLD – Australia's highest sand dune, Mount Tempest (280 m)
» Kaniaal Beach, WA – Australia's longest sand dune, extends 110 km inland.

Australia has the potential to become a destination for sand-boarding enthusiasts.

A string of half-sunken shipwrecks just off the beach at Tangalooma attracts curious divers and snorkellers. The beach is on the sheltered western coast of Moreton Island, a giant mass of sand that is now a national park just a short ferry ride from Brisbane.

TEA TREE BEACH NOOSA, QUEENSLAND

POCKET BEACH | SURFING | RAINFOREST WALKS | NOOSA CAFES AND RESTAURANTS

The popularity of Noosa's beaches and point breaks had its origins in the early 1960s when surfers came here seeking new waves. Those bands of adventurous surfers in beat-up cars, barefoot and broke, camped here and put beaches like Tea Tree and First Point on the front covers of magazines.

The walk from Noosa Beach to the eastward-protruding Noosa Head is probably the most popular 3-kilometre coastal walk in Australia. It takes in alternating boulder-rimmed headlands and curving pockets of sand, with superb surf breaks wrapping round the points and the dense rainforested slopes of the national park behind.

Leaving the main beach, you come to Little Cove, First Point, Witches Cauldron, Tea Tree, Dolphin Point, Granite Bay and the small Fairy Pools out near the point. Around the corner, is the longer more exposed Alexandria Bay, with the dramatic Hells Gate and Devils Kitchen on its boundary points. The best surf is at First Point, Tea Tree and Granite, which all offer the long easy waves that are a favourite with long-board riders. The four small beaches are popular with sunbathers, while nudists choose the more secluded Alexandria Bay.

There is also plenty of action in Noosa township and its main Hastings Street, which backs the main beach. The town, and neighbouring Noosaville and Tewantin, offer a wide range of accommodation and facilities. To the north is the Noosa River with its lakes and the long Cooloola beach, part of the Great Sandy National Park.

BEST NUDE BEACHES

If you want an all-over suntan, here are some beaches to head for:

» Alexandria Bay, Noosa, QLD
» Broken Head, NSW
» North Diggers, NSW
» Obelisk, Sydney Harbour, NSW
» Maslins, SA
» North Cable Beach, WA

There are dozens of 'free beaches' or clothing optional beaches in every state of Australia. Some are 'official' some 'unofficial' so it's a good idea to check the status. Also, follow the etiquette of nude bathing outlined by Free Beaches Australia.

Beautiful Tea Tree Beach is just one of the fine pocket beaches that dot the 3-kilometre coastal walk from Noosa Beach to Noosa Head, probably the most popular coastal walk in Australia. Tea Tree's long easy waves have been a favourite with long-board riders since the 1960s.

The calm waters of The Basin offer one of the best beach experiences on Rottnest Island, a short ferry ride from Perth. Visitors can snorkel over the shallow rock reefs or hop on a bike and explore the car-free roads of the island, with its 63 beaches and 20 bays.

THE BASIN

ROTTNEST ISLAND, WESTERN AUSTRALIA

CALM CLEAR WATERS | REEFS AND ROCK POOLS | SNORKELLING | CYCLING | QUOKKAS

The local name of Rotto just doesn't seem to do justice to this jewel of an island 20 kilometres off the West Australian coast and a half-hour ferry ride from Perth. Rottnest was named by the Dutch navigator Willem de Vlamingh when, in 1696, he mistook the native marsupial quokka for a rodent and thus called the place 'rat's nest'. Around 10 000 quokkas still call Rottnest home.

The island's history has not always been a happy one. In 1838, it was used as a penal colony for Aboriginal men and boys of the Noongar people, but in 1903 things took a turn for the better when it was declared a people's park, protecting it from over-development. Today it offers a range of accommodation scattered along its northern shore, with the bulk of the island still in a natural state.

One of the best of the many beaches is The Basin, near the ferry terminal and the island's only settlement of Thomsons Bay. Like most beaches on Rottnest it's short, only 200 metres long but, with its sunny northern aspect, calm, clear waters and shallow rock reefs dotted with deeper pools, The Basin offers wonderful swimming and snorkelling. A row of Norfolk Island pines, a shelter and picnic area stand on the backing bluffs.

If this is your first visit to Rottnest, the best way to tour the island is to hire a bike and explore its 63 beaches and 20 bays. With no private cars on the island, the 'roads' are all yours.

THE COORONG

LONG BEACH | WORLD HERITAGE | BIG DUNES | BIRDS | SEAGRASS MEADOWS

The World Heritage-listed Coorong is Australia's second-longest continuous beach (see Eighty Mile Beach) and one of its wildest. The only interruption along this seemingly endless 194-kilometre stretch of sand between Cape Jaffa and the mouth of the Murray River is two rounded lumps of rock known as The Granites about 20 kilometres north of the beach's only town, Kingston SE. Massive sand dunes right along the beach can extend inland by up to 2 kilometres.

Although the whole beach faces west into the prevailing winds and heavy south-west swell, the 22-kilometre southern section between Kingston and Cape Jaffa, known as Lacepede Bay, is almost entirely protected from the swell by submerged reefs and receives only local wind waves. This allows jetties to be maintained at Cape Jaffa and Kingston and for locals to launch boats directly off the beach. The calm conditions also allow seagrass to grow to the shore and you'll see it washed up on the beach.

The reef slowly deepens north of Kingston allowing more wave energy to reach shore. At The Granites, waves can average over 1 metre and by Tea Tree Crossing, 50 kilometres further north, the beach receives the full force of the Southern Ocean and waves average over 2.5 metres. The high waves continue for the next 100 kilometres until you reach the mouth of the Murray at Goolwa.

The name Coorong, meaning 'narrow neck' in the local Aboriginal language, refers to the salty lagoon that extends for 100 kilometres from Goolwa south behind the dunes, before breaking into a series of salt lakes that continue almost to Kingston. These lagoons and wetlands are home to over two hundred bird species, including migratory birds from as far away as Europe and Asia.

You can access the Coorong by car in the south, between Cape Jaffa and The Granites, or at Goolwa. With a 4WD you can visit the three 'crossings', at 28, 32 or 42 Mile, in the ecologically rich Coorong National Park. Experienced four-wheel drivers can drive the beach, although a permit is required and there are some seasonal closures to protect nesting birds.

At 194 kilometres, the World Heritage-listed Coorong is Australia's second longest continuous beach and one of its wildest. Although the beach faces west into the prevailing winds and heavy south-west swell, the southern section is protected by submerged reefs, allowing jetties to be maintained at Cape Jaffa and Kingston.

THE STRAND

CITY BEACH | HISTORIC BUILDINGS | LANDSCAPED PROMENADE | CHILDREN'S WATER PARK

Many visitors to Townsville take a ferry 7 kilometres offshore to Magnetic Island to enjoy the beaches there (see Horseshoe Bay). But now there is also a brilliantly designed and more accessible beach experience on the city's doorstep.

The Strand has been a part of Townsville's history since the city was founded in the mid-19th century. Many beautiful historical buildings dating back to early settlement line the foreshore, which is only 10 minutes from downtown Townsville. After the foreshore was ravaged by cyclones in the late 1990s, local, state and federal governments funded a spectacular new 'beach' here, pumping sand ashore to create a generous beach which opened to the applause of an 80 000 strong crowd in 1999.

Nestled on the shores of vast Cleveland Bay, The Strand has become one of Townsville's highlights – a 2.5-kilometre landscaped waterfront promenade that offers a model for urban foreshore developments in Australia. In a region that enjoys around 300 days of sunshine per year, The Strand is the social hub of the city.

Four rocky promontories break up the beach into five sections, providing space for the Townsville Surf Life Saving Club, restaurants, amenities and great views. The continuous wide foreshore reserve is studded with tropical palms and giant fig trees, and attracts locals and visitors wanting to relax, picnic, exercise or just soak up the views. It has a usually calm swimming beach with permanent stinger enclosures, a northern rock pool, a children's water park, extended viewing platforms, wide walkways and bike paths and a number of artistic and historic installations.

After the Townsville foreshore was ravaged by cyclones in the 1990s, authorities set about creating a new beach for the city. The resulting recreational space includes wide walkways, cycle paths, artworks, a rock pool and a children's water park.

The dramatic coastal landscape of Wilsons Promontery is dominated by towering granite peaks. The access road ends at Tidal River where a popular national park camping area sits behind the pristine beach.

TIDAL RIVER

WILSONS PROMONTORY, VICTORIA

DRAMATIC LANDSCAPE | NATIONAL PARK CAMPING | WALKS | NATURAL COAST | SEALS

Wilsons Promontory ends at South Cape, the southern tip of mainland Australia and 3200 kilometres, as the crow flies, from Cape York's Frangipani Beach, the country's northernmost beach (see Frangipani Beach).

The 'Prom' as Victorians prefer to call it, is one of the state's great natural destinations. Its dramatic coastal landscape is dominated by towering granite peaks, rising in places to 750 metres. It is surrounded by 120 kilometres of predominantly rocky granite shoreline, which contains 34, generally small, beaches, most accessible only on foot or by boat.

Explorers, sealers, whalers, timber-cutters, pastoralists, soldier settlers and goldminers all had an impact on the Prom before the declaration of the Wilsons Promontory National Park in 1905. The park is now surrounded by a series of marine parks.

The road to the Prom ends at Tidal River where you will find the large, very popular and well-maintained national park camping area set back from Norman Beach. From the campsite, follow one of the access tracks across the dunes to the beach where the fine silica sand has produced a wide firm beach with rows of waves usually breaking across the shallow surf zone. The beach is flanked by Pillar Point in the north and Norman Point in the south and offers dramatic views of Mount Oberon. If you climb the mountain, you will have panoramic views back to the beach. The two granite headlands extend 1 kilometre out to

sea, with a series of 100-metre-high, uninhabited islands dominating the horizon.

Most people stay at Tidal River but the Prom has a network of walking tracks and provides some great overnight camp sites, many at remote beaches like Sealers Cove and Refuge Cove (see Refuge Cove), both former whaling stations. You can also trek to small Home Cove, the southernmost mainland beach in Australia, and to the southern tip at South Point.

Closer to Tidal River are three smaller beaches – Squeaky Beach, Picnic Bay and Whisky Bay – all of which face west and are great for swimming, surfing, fishing or enjoying the sunset.

TROUSERS BEACH FLINDERS ISLAND, TASMANIA

ISLAND BEACH | BEACHCOMBING | WETLANDS | FISHING | CAMPING | SNORKELLING

Trousers is the best of the beaches on Flinders Island in Bass Strait. With its granite boulders sporting orange lichen, mostly calm waters and forested foredune, it is a peaceful place to swim, walk, snorkel or cast a fishing line.

Flinders is a magical island of natural coastal beauty and simple delights. The main island and the scatter of surrounding offshore islands or 'mountains in the sea', remained above the rising seas after the last ice age flooded Bass Strait. The island is not on many travellers' wish-lists, but it deserves to be.

The 234 kilometres of coast hosts 134 beaches, facing west into Bass Strait and east to the Tasman Sea and the best of them is Trousers Beach in the south-west corner. Tucked in behind Trousers Point, the beach curves to the south for 1.8 kilometres to Holts Point. The granite that forms the point rises east of the beach to the island's highest peak, the majestic Mount Strzelecki (765 metres).

There is a picnic area and a casuarina-sheltered camping area on the point. From here you can walk west to two small sheltered pocket beaches, both wedged between massive colourful sloping granite, with vibrant orange lichen covering the upper surfaces. Seagrass grows almost to the shore.

The main Trousers Beach (the name relates to a trouserless shipwrecked sailor), starts just below the car park. This is the most sheltered corner, with a wide low-gradient sandy beach and usually calm conditions. Waves gradually pick up as you move down the beach, with rip currents common along the southern half. A continuous well-vegetated foredune backs the beach, hiding a 45-hectare wetland, which only breaks out across the beach after heavy rain.

Trousers is a place to swim, snorkel, walk the beach and adjoining rocky points, fish and, camp under the bright stars. Flights from Melbourne and Launceston service Whitemark, the island's sleepy capital.

WARATAH BAY VICTORIA

UNDEVELOPED BEACH | SURFING | WILD STORMS | DUNES | HISTORIC RUINS | LIGHTHOUSE

Waratah Bay is a curving 26-kilometre-long bay washed by the waves that wrap around Cape Liptrap, its western point. The bay faces into Bass Strait and, except for the protected western end, receives the full force of the westerly storms. This relatively undeveloped spot is just off the South Gippsland Highway, a two-hour drive from Melbourne.

At the sheltered western corner is the historic Walkerville settlement now located in Cape Liptrap Coastal Park. The waves gradually increase in size as you move east, with good surf breaking across a 300-metre-wide surf zone that normally runs from the small centrally located Waratah Bay settlement along the beach to the slightly larger Sandy Point community and on to the wide, bare sand dunes of Sandy Point itself. The dunes continue for 5 kilometres to Shallow Inlet, where the tidal flow fights its way out through the wild surf. The small communities here are located behind the high foredune among the dense tea trees. Only the Waratah Bay Surf Life Saving Club is exposed to the ocean.

At Walkerville, the remains of limekilns, a tramway and a jetty can still be seen just behind the beach. They were in use between 1876 and 1926 when lime for building was shipped from here to the growing city of Melbourne. At Cape Liptrap, a lighthouse sits above steep cliffs of folded marine sediments flanked by rock pinnacles, wave-washed platforms and boulder beaches.

The long curving beach at Waratah Bay faces directly into Bass Strait and receives the full force of the westerly storms along most of its length. The small communities of Waratah Bay and Sandy Point take shelter in dense tea trees behind the high dunes.

WATEGOS BEACH
BYRON BAY, NEW SOUTH WALES

AUSTRALIA'S EASTERNMOST POINT | SURFING | HISTORIC LIGHTHOUSE | WHALES

Subtropical Wategos Beach nestles at the very tip of Cape Byron, making it the most easterly beach in Australia. Close to the lively township of Byron Bay, Wategos offers clear Pacific waters and good surf.

Subtropical Wategos Beach is nestled at the very tip of Cape Byron, making it the most easterly beach in Australia. The half-kilometre long strip of sand and rocks faces due north, with the 100-metre-high cape, topped by the historic Cape Byron Lighthouse, rising spectacularly behind.

The road from the town of Byron Bay winds along the northern side of the cape to reach the beach, which is set across the mouth of a small palm-filled valley. The beach is generally wide, with waves wrapping around the cape and running at an angle along the beach. The surf zone is usually shallow with good surf off the eastern rocks, popular with long-board and paddle-board riders. The waves can produce a sweep along the beach, so take care if swimming.

It's well worth making time to walk around the eastern rocks and along neighbouring Little Wategos Beach to the tip of the cape, the most easterly point on the Australian mainland. Then walk up the track, or drive, to the lighthouse for

a breath-taking view south along Tallows Beach to Broken Head, north over the diver's paradise of Julian Rocks and inland to Mount Warning, which was so named by Captain James Cook. In season, this is also a popular whale-watching site. The whole area is rich in Aboriginal history. The site of the lighthouse was once used as a ceremonial dancing circle and Tallows Beach, rich in shell middens, is the site of the last Aboriginal camp in the area. You can also walk west out along the rocks or paddle around the corner to The Pass, another glorious surfing spot.

The valley behind Wategos Beach was first occupied by the Watego family in the 1930s. But from the late 1950s the local shire council, wanting to develop the area, set up a lottery system and began to give away land on the condition that new landholders must clear the land for building within two years. The value of land here now – some of it originally acquired via the lottery – ranks among the highest anywhere on the Australian coast.

BEST LIGHTHOUSE BEACH VIEWS

Lighthouses always occupy prominent positions and often provide spectacular views of adjoining beaches. Some of the best views are from:

» Sugarloaf Point, NSW – Lighthouse Beach
» Cape DuCouedic, Kangaroo Island, SA – Sanderson Bay
» Smoky Cape, NSW – Smoky Cape Beach
» Cape Byron, NSW – Tallows Beach
» Barrenjoey, NSW – Palm Beach
» Cape Moreton, QLD – Honeymoon Bay

Many lighthouses now offer accommodation in the former lighthouse keepers' cottages.

WESTERN RIVER COVE
KANGAROO ISLAND, SOUTH AUSTRALIA

ISLAND BEACH | SNORKELLING | RUGGED COAST | PIRATE HISTORY

Seal hunters used Kangaroo Island as a base long before any planned settlement began, but the island remained sparsely populated until some of the land was assigned to soldier settlers after WWII. It now has a population of 4500, mostly located in Kingscote and Penneshaw.

The remainder of this hilly island remains sparsely populated particularly along the coast. The whole western end of the island is included in the Flinders Chase National Park.

Typical of the rugged north coast is Western River Cove, a 150-metre-long strip of sand that blocks a small river mouth. The quiet Western River, more often a dry creek, winds down through the backing slopes to reach the cove, which is protected by headlands formed of vertically dipping rock strata, contorted by plate tectonics. The headlands are just 200 metres apart and enclose the main beach as well as a second 40-m-long boulder beach wedged against the eastern headland.

The gravel access road winds down the slopes to a car park, picnic shelter and small camping area overlooking the river. A footbridge provides access to the beach track across the shallow river. The short track brings you to the hidden cove, which local lore says was the haunt of colonial pirates.

The waves here are usually calm or low, washing up a moderately steep beach that drops into deeper water. Fishing boats sometimes anchor here, pulling their dinghies up onto the sand. The beach is ideal for fishing, swimming, snorkelling or diving around the adjacent headlands and reefs. You can also walk along their rugged rock platforms at the base of the headlands, but watch your footing. Behind the beach, an active sand dune extends as far as the footbridge.

On the rugged north coast of Kangaroo Island, Western River Cove is sheltered by two headlands just 200 metres apart. Fishing boats sometimes anchor here and the calm wateres are ideal for swimming, snorkelling or diving around the adjacent headlands and reefs.

WHITEHAVEN BEACH
WHITSUNDAY ISLAND, QUEENSLAND

WHITE SANDS | SAILING | SNORKELLING | INLET WALKS | ISLAND BEACH | NATIONAL PARK

This island beach really lives up to its name. It boasts pure white sand and is also renowned as a safe haven for yachts and boats, which lie at anchor off its sheltered southern shores in the lee of Haslewood Island.

Whitehaven is located on Whitsunday Island and is part of the Whitsunday Islands National Park, which contains another eight islands all surrounded by a marine park. Whitehaven is the most popular of the local beaches and is visited by boatloads of beach lovers everyday.

If you land at high tide, you will find a pure white 50-metre-wide strip of sand backed by a densely vegetated foredune. At low tide, you will encounter a shallow sandbar, with tropical seagrasses growing just a few metres from the shore. Low tide is also when the charter flights by seaplane or helicopter come in to land. While most visitors come just for the day, there are campsites in the vine and woodland forest behind the beach, as well as shelters and picnic areas.

The beach is unusual for the Whitsundays in a number of ways. Its sand is pure silica and thus pure white whereas most of the surrounding islands and beaches have a high proportion of darker carbonate sands derived from the fringing coral reefs. Whitehaven Beach is also long, nearly 6 kilometres, when many others are less than 100 metres. It also boasts the stunning Hill Inlet at its northern end, where the tide shifts the white sand and turquoise water to form intricate shoal patterns in a beautiful fusion of colours. For the best view, charter a plane or journey to the lookout at Tongue Point at low tide when the patterns and colours are most vibrant.

Whitehaven Beach on Whitsunday Island is one of several beaches to claim the title of whitest sands in Australia. At the northern end of the beach is the stunning Hill Inlet, where the tide shifts the turquoise water and white sands to create a superb play of colours.

WHITEST SAND

Australia's whitest beaches are all composed of pure white silica sand, free of impurities. Three widely separated beaches could claim this title:

» Whitehaven Beach, QLD
» Green Patch, Jervis Bay Territory
» Lucky Bay, WA

You be the judge, but take your sunnies as the glare is blinding.

WINEGLASS BAY
FREYCINET PENINSULA, TASMANIA

COASTAL WALKS | WHITE SANDS | DEEP WATERS | NATIONAL PARK | WETLANDS | BIRD LIFE

Wineglass Bay in the magnificent Freycinet National Park is Tasmania's most photographed beach and has become one of Australia's most popular tourist destinations. Each year, 150 000 visitors make the 30-minute walk up the track to Hazards Lookout to photograph the unparalleled beach vista.

The beach forms the eastern side of a 1.5-kilometre-wide low, vegetated isthmus that connects Freycinet Peninsula to the mainland, all within the national park.

The area's history is reflected in the names given by the early Dutch explorers (Schouten and Maria islands), then the French (Freycinet, Cape Tourville and Point Geographe) and finally the early Welsh settlers (Swansea and Glamorgan).

If you have time, there is a circuit walk from Wineglass Bay across to Hazards Beach and then back around the western slopes of the Hazards, pausing at Lemana Lookout for a breathtaking view back along Hazards Beach. Between the beaches is a wetland that attracts many of the birds the area is renowned for. A checklist of 114 bird species is available from the Tasmanian Parks Service.

For the more adventurous, the three-day Freycinet Peninsula circuit walk begins at the Wineglass Bay campsite in the southern, sheltered corner of the beach next to Indigo Creek.

Down on the beach at Wineglass Bay, the sand is pure white silica eroded from the surrounding granite rocks. The beach is soft and steep and lined with crescentic beach cusps – hollows and ridges in the high-tide beach formed by the surging swash that extends the length of the beach. The beach curves symmetrically for 1.7 kilometres and usually has low waves washing up against the steep face, with deep clear water just off the beach. If you've worked up a sweat trekking, this is a great place to cool off with a refreshing swim.

MOST PHOTOGRAPHED

The clear skies, sparkling water and sweeping sands of Australian beaches attract photographers from everywhere. Some of their favourites are:

» Wineglass Bay, TAS
» Bondi Beach, NSW
» Whitehaven Beach, QLD
» The Twelve Apostles, VIC
» Lucky Bay, WA
» Seventeen-Seventy, QLD

Of course not all great photographs need clear skies and sunshine – some of the most stunning show wild surf and windswept sand.

The starting point for the three-day Freycinet Peninsula circuit walk, Wineglass Bay is one of the most beautiful and most photographed beaches in Australia. A wetland behind the beach attracts many of the birds the area is renowned for.

WINGAN INLET EAST GIPPSLAND, VICTORIA

NATURAL COAST | BUSH CAMPING | TALL GUMS | LAGOON | WALKS | FUR SEALS

East Gippsland's Wingan Inlet hides deep in the forested corners of Croajingolong National Park at the end of a 34-kilometre-long gravel track off the Princes Highway. The drive in from the highway, which can take up to an hour, winds through tall eucalypts to a forested picnic and camping area beside the clear, shallow Wingan Lagoon about 1 kilometre back from the beach. This beautiful, pristine estuary is a favourite with nature lovers, hikers, surfers and fishers.

To reach the beach from the campsite follow the Wingan Nature Walk through the forest and on to an elevated wooden boardwalk across the melaleuca swamp. Continue up and over the foredune to the usually deserted beach that stretches for 1 kilometre in either direction.

Heading east towards the inlet, you will find surf, gutters for fishing and, out on the 'Skerries' – a rock reef off the eastern headland – a colony of fur-seals. To the west, the waves gradually decrease in the shelter of Rame Head.

In 1797, maritime explorers George Bass and Matthew Flinders anchored their open whaleboat here, naming the corner 'Fly Cove'. A small, attached island shelters the cove, which they would probably find unchanged today. This more sheltered end is popular with families.

There are about 20 shady campsites at Wingan and bookings though Parks Victoria are essential during holiday periods. Even during busy times, you are unlikely to find more than 100 people enjoying this superb natural environment with its meandering river, lagoon and inlet, the beach and bordering granite headlands. The Wilderness Coast Walk, which runs from Sydenham Inlet to Wonboyn in New South Wales, crosses the beach, with walkers either wading the narrow inlet at low tide or hitching a ride across.

Bring everything you need because facilities are limited. And if you really want to make the best of this magnificent inlet and park bring a boat.

The pristine surf beach and lagoon at Wingan Inlet hides deep in the forests of Croajingolong National Park, East Gippsland. An elevated boardwalk through the melaleuca swamp links the forest camping area to the beach.

ACKNOWLEDGMENTS

When you set out to find Australia's best beaches you have to put a lot of sand between your toes. In making sure that all of the information on the beaches was up to date we travelled over a period of three months from Cape Tribulation in north Queensland right round to Green Head, halfway up the Western Australian coast, plus all round Tasmania and the islands. To achieve all this in a relatively short space of time we received generous assistance from a variety of people and businesses, who all loved the idea.

For assistance in travels we sincerely thank Britz Motorhomes (Sally Wells and Sharon Clark) for providing comfortable motorhomes for travel in Tasmania and southeast Australia; Norfolk Island Tourism (Tania Anderson and Linda Muossa) for their overwhelming hospitality; Tourism Australia (Emma Sturgiss) for support throughout; Tourism Queensland (Bruce Wallace), Tourism Tasmania (Josh Iles) and Tourism Western Australia (Sarah Monahan and Kelly Townson) for welcoming help in visiting their states.

For generous assistance with accommodation we thank Ferntree Lodge (Cape Tribulation); Peninsula Boutique Beach Resort (Port Douglas); Eco Village Resort at Mission Beach (Dan and Uncle Dan); Cape Hillsborough Nature Resort (Marilyn); Sandcastles 1770 (Agnes Waters, Antony O'Dwyer); Karma Chalets (Denmark); Smith Beach Resort (Smith Beach, Tony Fletcher); Eaglehawk Dive Centre Pirates Bay; and Paradise Hotel and Resort, Norfolk Island (Sandy and Simon Pettit).

For general hospitality we thank the people of Norfolk and Flinders Islands, Adam Karras at Elandra Resort and Don Stayte at Eimeo Pacific Hotel.

For checking and comments on parts of the manuscript we thank Drew Kampion, Tim Baker and Norm Farmer, for reading and commenting on the entire manuscript and assisting in much of the beach checking we thank Julia Short. We're indebted to the generosity of many passionate photographers and to thousands of genuinely helpful folk, who've shared their beach and their stories with us along the way.

Brad extends special thanks to the Hall family, Sean Doherty, James 'Blondz' Alcock, Tyler Luck, Stephen O'Brien, Kelly Slater, Wayne 'Rabbit' Bartholomew AM, Surfrider Foundation Australia and to Nikon for the aptly named 'Coolpix' P7000.

At NewSouth Publishing we thank Jane McCredie for bringing our idea to life, her unfailing enthusiasm and convincing us we needed to go back to the beaches one more time and for publishing the manuscript so ably; Dr Heather Cam the managing editor for having faith in the idea; Melita Rogowsky for overseeing the project; Josephine Pajor-Markus for the overall design and page layout; and Averil Moffat for editing the entire manuscript. Thanks to a very dedicated and talented team to achieve a great result, a benchmark for Australia's best beaches.

Finally, thanks to you the reader and all beach-lovers who care for our coast and are entrusted with its future.

PHOTOGRAPHIC CREDITS

INDEX

BEST BEACHES BY STATE

QUEENSLAND